Harmony in the Digital Jungle: Unveiling the Secrets of Home-Based Success

imed el arbi

Published by imed el arbi, 2023.

While every precaution has been taken in the preparation of this book, the publisher assumes no responsibility for errors or omissions, or for damages resulting from the use of the information contained herein.

HARMONY IN THE DIGITAL JUNGLE: UNVEILING THE SECRETS OF HOME-BASED SUCCESS

First edition. November 18, 2023.

Written by imed el arbi.

Table of Contents

Harmony in the Digital Jungle

Unveiling the Secrets of Home-Based Success

IMED EL ARBI

EVERY DAY, A MULTITUDE sets sail into the uncharted realms of working from home, weaving dreams of independent ventures and untethered aspirations. The echo of success stories, some soaring to ethereal heights, fuels their imagination and propels them into the boundless landscape of possibility. In this vast expanse of the Internet, where the traditional markers of education fade into insignificance, a universal truth emerges. The common thread binding those who carve a path to success from the comforts of home is not the accolades of academia but the essence of character—their innate ability to become self-starters in the face of uncertainty. Imagine the digital realm as a jungle, teeming with opportunities and challenges alike. Those who thrive possess an unyielding positivity, an unwavering willingness to learn, and an arsenal of survival skills finely honed in the crucible of the online wilderness. So, if you find yourself contemplating the plunge into the enigmatic world of home-based endeavors, you are already a self-starter, an adventurer traversing uncharted territories. Your positive outlook has led you to this juncture, and the fact that you're reading these lines signals your readiness to learn and navigate the intricate paths of the digital jungle. "Harmony in the Digital Jungle" invites you to explore the emotional tapestry of those who dare to dream beyond the conventional. It's a poetic journey that celebrates the spirit of self-starters, the optimism that lights the way, and the resilience required to master survival skills in this vast, ever-changing landscape of virtual existence. Welcome to the symphony of success, where formal education takes a back seat to the melody of determination, innovation, and the pursuit of dreams.

The Rise of the Digital Jungle

1.1 Understanding the Digital Landscape

In today's fast-paced and interconnected world, the digital landscape has become a thriving jungle of opportunities for home-based entrepreneurs. The rise of the internet and the widespread adoption of technology have transformed the way we live, work, and do business. To navigate this digital jungle successfully, it is crucial to understand the intricacies of the digital landscape and how it can impact your home-based business.

1.1.1 The Evolution of the Digital Landscape

THE DIGITAL LANDSCAPE has evolved significantly over the years, revolutionizing the way we communicate, access information, and conduct business. With the advent of the internet, the world has become more connected than ever before. The rise of social media platforms, e-commerce websites, and online marketplaces further accelerated this transformation, creating a vast digital ecosystem where businesses of all sizes can thrive.

1.1.2 The Power of the Internet

THE INTERNET HAS BECOME an integral part of our daily lives, offering endless possibilities for entrepreneurs to establish and grow their home-based businesses. It has leveled the playing field, allowing small businesses to compete with larger corporations on a global scale. The internet provides a platform for entrepreneurs to showcase their products or services, reach a wider audience, and engage with customers in real-time.

1.1.3 The Influence of Technology

TECHNOLOGY PLAYS A pivotal role in shaping the digital landscape. From smartphones and tablets to cloud computing and artificial intelligence, technological advancements have revolutionized the way we work and interact with the digital world. These innovations have made it easier for home-based entrepreneurs to manage their businesses, automate processes, and stay connected with customers and clients.

1.1.4 The Rise of E-Commerce

E-COMMERCE HAS EMERGED as a dominant force in the digital landscape, transforming the way businesses sell and consumers shop. Online marketplaces like Amazon, eBay, and Etsy have provided a platform for home-based entrepreneurs to showcase their products to a global audience. The convenience and accessibility of online shopping have fueled the growth of e-commerce, making it an essential component of any successful home-based business.

1.1.5 The Impact of Social Media

SOCIAL MEDIA PLATFORMS have revolutionized the way we connect, communicate, and consume information. These platforms, such as Facebook, Instagram, Twitter, and LinkedIn, have become powerful marketing tools for home-based entrepreneurs. They allow businesses to build brand awareness, engage with customers, and drive traffic to their websites. Social media also provides valuable insights into consumer behavior and preferences, enabling businesses to tailor their marketing strategies accordingly.

1.1.6 The Importance of Online Presence

IN THE DIGITAL LANDSCAPE, having a strong online presence is crucial for the success of any home-based business. A professional website serves as a virtual storefront, showcasing your products or services and providing essential information to potential customers. Optimizing your website for search engines ensures that your business is visible to those searching for relevant keywords. Engaging content, such as blog posts and videos, helps establish your expertise and build trust with your audience.

1.1.7 The Need for Adaptability

THE DIGITAL LANDSCAPE is constantly evolving, and home-based entrepreneurs must be adaptable to stay ahead of the competition. New technologies, trends, and consumer behaviors emerge regularly, requiring businesses to embrace change and adapt their strategies accordingly. By staying informed and continuously learning, entrepreneurs can leverage the digital landscape to their advantage and seize new opportunities as they arise.

1.1.8 The Challenges of the Digital Landscape

WHILE THE DIGITAL LANDSCAPE offers immense opportunities, it also presents unique challenges for home-based entrepreneurs. The rapid pace of technological advancements can be overwhelming, making it difficult to keep up with the latest trends and tools. The digital landscape is also highly competitive, requiring businesses to differentiate themselves and stand out from the crowd. Additionally, cybersecurity threats and online scams pose risks that entrepreneurs must be aware of and protect against.

1.1.9 Embracing the Digital Landscape

TO THRIVE IN THE DIGITAL jungle, home-based entrepreneurs must embrace the digital landscape and leverage its power to their advantage. This requires a deep understanding of evolving technologies, consumer behaviors, and market trends. By staying informed, adapting to change, and utilizing the right tools and strategies, entrepreneurs can unlock the secrets of home-based success in the digital age.

In the next chapter, we will explore the strategies for building a strong foundation for your home-based business, including defining your business, setting goals, and establishing your brand identity.

1.2 Navigating the Online Marketplace

IN TODAY'S DIGITAL age, the online marketplace has become a vast and complex ecosystem. Navigating this digital jungle can be overwhelming, especially for home-based entrepreneurs who are just starting their journey. However, with the right knowledge and strategies, you can successfully navigate the online marketplace and thrive in your home-based business.

1.2.1 Understanding the Online Marketplace

BEFORE DIVING INTO the online marketplace, it is crucial to understand its dynamics and how it operates. The online marketplace refers to the virtual space where buyers and sellers interact to exchange goods and services. It encompasses various platforms, such as e-commerce websites, social media platforms, online marketplaces, and search engines.

One of the key aspects of the online marketplace is the concept of e-commerce. E-commerce involves the buying and selling of products or services over the internet. It has revolutionized the way businesses operate, providing opportunities for entrepreneurs to reach a global audience from the comfort of their homes.

1.2.2 Identifying Your Target Market

TO NAVIGATE THE ONLINE marketplace effectively, you need to identify your target market. Your target market consists of a specific group of people who are most likely to be interested in your products or services. Understanding your target market allows you to tailor your marketing efforts and offerings to meet their needs and preferences.

To identify your target market, you can conduct market research to gather information about your potential customers. This research can include analyzing demographics, psychographics, and consumer behavior. By understanding your target market's characteristics, interests, and purchasing habits, you can develop effective marketing strategies and position your business in the online marketplace.

1.2.3 Building an Online Presence

ESTABLISHING A STRONG online presence is essential for navigating the online marketplace successfully. Your online presence is the digital representation of your brand and business. It includes your website, social media profiles, online listings, and any other online platforms where your business is visible.

To build an effective online presence, you need to create a professional website that showcases your products or services. Your website should be visually appealing, user-friendly, and optimized for search engines. Additionally, you should leverage social media platforms to engage with your target market, share valuable content, and promote your offerings.

1.2.4 Utilizing Online Marketing Strategies

IN THE ONLINE MARKETPLACE, marketing plays a crucial role in attracting and retaining customers. Online marketing strategies allow you to reach a wider audience, increase brand awareness, and drive traffic to your website.

Some effective online marketing strategies include search engine optimization (SEO), content marketing, social media marketing, and email marketing.

SEO involves optimizing your website and content to rank higher in search engine results. By incorporating relevant keywords, creating high-quality content, and building backlinks, you can improve your website's visibility and attract organic traffic.

Content marketing focuses on creating and sharing valuable content to attract and engage your target audience. This can include blog posts, videos, infographics, and podcasts. By providing valuable information and addressing your audience's pain points, you can establish yourself as an authority in your industry and build trust with your potential customers.

Social media marketing involves leveraging social media platforms to promote your brand and engage with your audience. By creating compelling content, running targeted ads, and interacting with your followers, you can increase brand awareness and drive traffic to your website.

Email marketing is another effective strategy for nurturing relationships with your audience and driving sales. By building an email list and sending targeted and personalized emails, you can keep your audience informed about your latest offerings, promotions, and updates.

1.2.5 Monitoring and Analyzing Performance

TO NAVIGATE THE ONLINE marketplace effectively, it is crucial to monitor and analyze your business's performance. By tracking key metrics and analyzing data, you can gain insights into your customers' behavior, the effectiveness of your marketing strategies, and the overall performance of your business.

There are various tools and platforms available that can help you monitor and analyze your online performance. Google Analytics, for example, provides valuable insights into website traffic, user behavior, and conversion rates. Social media analytics tools allow you to track engagement, reach, and audience demographics on social media platforms.

By regularly reviewing and analyzing your performance data, you can identify areas for improvement, make data-driven decisions, and optimize your strategies to achieve better results in the online marketplace.

1.2.6 Staying Updated with Trends and Innovations

THE ONLINE MARKETPLACE is constantly evolving, with new trends and innovations emerging regularly. To stay ahead of the competition and navigate the digital jungle successfully, it is essential to stay updated with the latest trends and innovations in your industry.

Subscribe to industry newsletters, follow influential thought leaders, and participate in online communities and forums related to your niche. By staying informed about industry trends, consumer preferences, and technological advancements, you can adapt your strategies and offerings to meet the changing demands of the online marketplace.

In conclusion, navigating the online marketplace requires a deep understanding of its dynamics, identifying your target market, building a strong online presence, utilizing effective marketing strategies, monitoring performance, and staying updated with trends and innovations. By implementing these strategies and continuously learning and adapting, you can navigate the digital jungle with confidence and achieve home-based success.

1.3 Embracing the Digital Revolution

IN TODAY'S FAST-PACED and interconnected world, the digital revolution has transformed the way we live, work, and do business. The rise of the internet and advancements in technology have created a digital jungle, a vast and ever-expanding landscape where opportunities abound for home-based entrepreneurs. Embracing the digital revolution is not only essential for survival in this new business environment but also a key factor in achieving home-based success.

1.3.1 The Power of the Digital Revolution

THE DIGITAL REVOLUTION has brought about a paradigm shift in the way businesses operate. It has leveled the playing field, allowing home-based entrepreneurs to compete with larger, more established companies. The barriers to entry have been significantly reduced, enabling individuals to start their own businesses from the comfort of their homes with minimal upfront costs.

One of the most significant advantages of the digital revolution is the ability to reach a global audience. With the internet, geographical boundaries are no longer a limitation. Home-based entrepreneurs can now connect with customers from all over the world, expanding their market reach and potential customer base exponentially.

Furthermore, the digital revolution has revolutionized the way products and services are delivered. E-commerce platforms have made it easier than ever to sell products online, eliminating the need for a physical storefront. Digital products, such as e-books, online courses, and software, can be created and distributed instantly, providing a scalable and profitable business model for home-based entrepreneurs.

1.3.2 Harnessing the Tools of the Digital Revolution

TO FULLY EMBRACE THE digital revolution, home-based entrepreneurs must harness the power of the tools and technologies available to them. These tools not only streamline business operations but also enhance productivity and efficiency.

One of the essential tools for home-based entrepreneurs is a reliable internet connection. It serves as the backbone of the digital business, enabling communication, research, and online transactions. Investing in a high-speed internet connection is crucial for seamless operations and an effective online presence.

Another vital tool is a computer or laptop. It serves as the primary device for conducting business activities, such as creating content, managing finances, and communicating with clients. Investing in a reliable and up-to-date computer is essential for smooth workflow and productivity.

In addition to hardware, there are numerous software applications and online platforms that can greatly benefit home-based entrepreneurs. Project management tools, such as

Trello or Asana, help in organizing tasks and collaborating with team members. Customer relationship management (CRM) software, like Salesforce or HubSpot, assists in managing customer interactions and sales processes. Social media management tools, such as Hootsuite or Buffer, streamline social media marketing efforts. These tools, among many others, can significantly enhance productivity and efficiency in a home-based business.

1.3.3 Adapting to the Changing Business Landscape

THE DIGITAL REVOLUTION has not only brought opportunities but also challenges. Home-based entrepreneurs must be adaptable and willing to embrace change to thrive in this ever-evolving business landscape.

One of the key aspects of adapting to the changing business landscape is staying updated with the latest trends and technologies. The digital world is constantly evolving, and new tools and strategies emerge regularly. Home-based entrepreneurs must invest time and effort in continuous learning and professional development to stay ahead of the curve.

Additionally, embracing the digital revolution requires a mindset shift. Traditional business models and practices may no longer be effective in the digital jungle. Home-based entrepreneurs must be open to new ideas, innovative approaches, and unconventional strategies. Embracing a growth mindset and being willing to experiment and take calculated risks are essential for success in the digital era.

Furthermore, building a strong online presence is crucial for home-based entrepreneurs. This includes having a professional website, utilizing social media platforms, and creating engaging content. Establishing a strong online brand and reputation is essential for attracting and retaining customers in the digital landscape.

1.3.4 The Future of Home-Based Success

THE DIGITAL REVOLUTION shows no signs of slowing down. As technology continues to advance, new opportunities and challenges will arise for home-based entrepreneurs. Embracing the digital revolution is not a one-time event but an ongoing process of adaptation and innovation.

Home-based entrepreneurs who embrace the digital revolution and leverage the power of technology will be well-positioned for success in the future. By staying updated with the latest trends, harnessing the tools of the digital revolution, and adapting to the changing business landscape, they can navigate the digital jungle with confidence and achieve home-based success.

In the following chapters, we will delve deeper into the strategies and techniques that will help you build a strong foundation, master time and productivity, implement effective marketing and promotion strategies, build an online presence, manage finances and taxes, build a supportive network, and overcome challenges on your journey to home-based success.

Building a Strong Foundation

2.1 Defining Your Home-Based Business

In order to build a strong foundation for your home-based business, it is crucial to clearly define what your business is all about. Defining your home-based business involves identifying your niche, understanding your target market, and determining the products or services you will offer. This section will guide you through the process of defining your home-based business and help you lay the groundwork for success.

2.1.1 Identifying Your Niche

ONE OF THE FIRST STEPS in defining your home-based business is identifying your niche. A niche is a specific area or market segment that you will focus on. By narrowing down your focus, you can differentiate yourself from competitors and target a specific audience that is more likely to be interested in what you have to offer.

To identify your niche, start by considering your interests, skills, and expertise. What are you passionate about? What are you knowledgeable in? By aligning your business with your passions and expertise, you will not only enjoy what you do but also have a competitive advantage.

Additionally, research the market to identify gaps or underserved areas. Look for opportunities where you can provide unique solutions or products. By catering to a specific niche, you can position yourself as an expert and attract customers who are specifically looking for what you offer.

2.1.2 Understanding Your Target Market

ONCE YOU HAVE IDENTIFIED your niche, it is essential to understand your target market. Your target market consists of a specific group of people who are most likely to be interested in your products or services. Understanding your target market will help you tailor your marketing efforts and effectively reach your potential customers.

To understand your target market, conduct market research. This can involve analyzing demographic information such as age, gender, location, and income level. It can also involve studying psychographic factors such as interests, values, and lifestyle choices. By gathering this information, you can create buyer personas that represent your ideal customers and guide your marketing strategies.

In addition to demographic and psychographic factors, consider the needs and pain points of your target market. What problems do they have that your products or services can solve? By understanding their needs, you can position your business as a solution provider and effectively communicate the value you offer.

2.1.3 Determining Your Products or Services

ONCE YOU HAVE IDENTIFIED your niche and understood your target market, it is time to determine the products or services you will offer. This step is crucial, as it forms the core of your home-based business.

Start by brainstorming ideas based on your niche and the needs of your target market. Consider your skills, expertise, and resources. What can you offer that will provide value to your customers? Think about how you can differentiate your products or services from competitors and offer something unique.

Next, evaluate the feasibility and profitability of your ideas. Conduct market research to determine if there is demand for your products or services. Assess the competition and identify any potential barriers to entry. Consider the cost of production, pricing strategies, and potential profit margins.

Once you have determined your products or services, it is important to clearly define their features and benefits. What makes your offerings stand out? How will they solve the problems or meet the needs of your target market? Clearly articulating the value of your products or services will help you effectively market and sell them.

2.1.4 Crafting Your Unique Selling Proposition

IN A COMPETITIVE MARKETPLACE, it is essential to differentiate yourself from competitors and clearly communicate why customers should choose your business. This is where your unique selling proposition (USP) comes into play. Your USP is a concise statement that highlights the unique benefits or advantages of your products or services.

To craft your USP, consider the following questions:

1. What makes your products or services different from competitors?
2. What specific benefits do your offerings provide to customers?
3. How do your offerings solve the problems or meet the needs of your target market?
4. Why should customers choose your business over others?

By answering these questions, you can create a compelling USP that sets your home-based business apart. Your USP should be clear, concise, and memorable. It should effectively communicate the value you offer and resonate with your target market.

In conclusion, defining your home-based business is a crucial step in building a strong foundation for success. By identifying your niche, understanding your target market, determining your products or services, and crafting your unique selling proposition, you can position your business for growth and profitability. Take the time to carefully define your home-based business, as it will serve as a roadmap for your future endeavors.

2.2 Setting Goals and Objectives

SETTING CLEAR GOALS and objectives is a crucial step in building a strong foundation for your home-based business.

Without a clear direction and purpose, it can be easy to get lost in the vast digital jungle. In this section, we will explore the importance of setting goals and objectives and provide practical tips on how to do so effectively.

2.2.1 The Power of Goals

GOALS SERVE AS A ROADMAP for your business. They provide a sense of direction and purpose, helping you stay focused and motivated. By setting specific, measurable, achievable, relevant, and time-bound (SMART) goals, you can create a clear path towards success.

Specific

WHEN SETTING GOALS, it's important to be specific about what you want to achieve. Vague goals such as "increase sales" or "grow my business" lack clarity and make it difficult to measure progress. Instead, define your goals in specific terms. For example, "increase monthly sales by 20% within the next six months" provides a clear target to work towards.

Measurable

MEASURING PROGRESS is essential to tracking your success and making adjustments along the way. By setting measurable goals, you can quantify your achievements and determine whether you're on track. For instance, if your goal is to acquire 100 new customers in a month, you can easily measure your progress by tracking the number of new customers you've gained.

Achievable

WHILE IT'S IMPORTANT to set ambitious goals, they should also be realistic and attainable. Setting unattainable goals can lead to frustration and demotivation. Consider your available resources, skills, and market conditions when setting goals. It's better to set smaller, achievable goals that can be built upon over time than to set lofty goals that are unlikely to be reached.

Relevant

GOALS SHOULD BE ALIGNED with your overall vision and mission. They should be relevant to your business and contribute to its growth and success. Before setting goals, evaluate how they align with your long-term objectives. If a goal doesn't directly contribute to your business's success, it may be worth reconsidering or modifying it.

Time-Bound

SETTING A TIMEFRAME for your goals adds a sense of urgency and helps you stay focused. Without a deadline, goals can easily be pushed aside or forgotten. By setting specific timeframes, you create a sense of accountability and ensure that you're actively working towards achieving your goals.

2.2.2 Types of Goals

WHEN SETTING GOALS for your home-based business, it's helpful to consider different types of goals that can guide your actions and measure your progress. Here are some common types of goals to consider:

Financial Goals

FINANCIAL GOALS FOCUS on the financial aspects of your business, such as revenue, profit, and cash flow. Examples of financial goals include increasing sales, improving profit margins, or reducing expenses. These goals are essential for the sustainability and growth of your business.

Marketing Goals

MARKETING GOALS REVOLVE around promoting your products or services and reaching your target audience. Examples of marketing goals include increasing website traffic, growing social media followers, or improving conversion rates. These goals help you build brand awareness and attract potential customers.

Personal Development Goals

PERSONAL DEVELOPMENT goals focus on improving your skills and knowledge as a business owner. Examples of personal development goals include attending industry conferences, completing online courses, or joining professional networks. These goals contribute to your personal growth and enhance your ability to run a successful home-based business.

Customer service goals

CUSTOMER SERVICE GOALS aim to provide exceptional service and satisfaction to your customers. Examples of customer service goals include reducing response times, increasing customer retention rates, or improving online reviews. These goals help build customer loyalty and enhance your business's reputation.

Social Impact Goals

SOCIAL IMPACT GOALS focus on making a positive difference in society or the environment. Examples of social impact goals include implementing sustainable practices, supporting local communities, or donating a percentage of profits to charitable causes. These goals align your business with social responsibility and can attract socially conscious customers.

2.2.3 Setting Effective Goals and Objectives

NOW THAT YOU UNDERSTAND the importance of setting goals and the different types of goals to consider, let's explore some practical tips for setting effective goals and objectives for your home-based business:

1. Start with your vision and mission.

YOUR GOALS SHOULD ALIGN with your overall vision and mission for your business. Consider what you want to achieve in the long term and how your goals can contribute to that vision. This will ensure that your goals are meaningful and relevant to your business's success.

2. Break down long-term goals into short-term objectives.

LONG-TERM GOALS CAN feel overwhelming, so it's helpful to break them down into smaller, manageable objectives. By setting short-term objectives, you can track your progress more effectively and stay motivated along the way. Each objective should contribute to the achievement of your long-term goals.

3. Prioritize your goals.

NOT ALL GOALS ARE EQUALLY important or urgent. Prioritize your goals based on their impact on your business and the resources required to achieve them. Focus on the goals that will have the most significant positive impact and work towards them first. This will help you stay focused and avoid spreading yourself too thin.

4. Make your goals specific and measurable.

ENSURE THAT YOUR GOALS are specific and measurable so that you can track your progress and determine whether you've achieved them. Use metrics and key performance indicators (KPIs) to quantify your goals and establish a baseline for measurement. This will provide clarity and enable you to make data-driven decisions.

5. Review and adjust your goals regularly.

AS YOUR BUSINESS EVOLVES and market conditions change, it's important to review and adjust your goals accordingly. Regularly assess your progress and make necessary adjustments to keep your goals relevant and attainable. Flexibility and adaptability are key to staying on track and achieving long-term success.

By setting clear goals and objectives for your home-based business, you lay the foundation for success. Goals provide direction, motivation, and a sense of purpose, helping you navigate the digital jungle with confidence. Remember to make your goals smart, consider different types of goals, and regularly review and adjust them as needed. With a clear roadmap in place, you'll be well on your way to achieving harmony in the digital jungle and unlocking the secrets of home-based success.

2.4 Establishing Your Brand Identity

IN THE VAST AND COMPETITIVE digital landscape, establishing a strong brand identity is crucial for the success of your home-based business. Your brand identity is what sets you apart from your competitors and helps you connect with your target audience on a deeper level. It encompasses the visual elements, messaging, and values that define your business and shape how it is perceived by others. In this section, we will explore the key steps to effectively establish your brand identity and create a lasting impression in the digital jungle.

2.4.1 Defining Your Brand

BEFORE YOU CAN ESTABLISH your brand identity, you need to have a clear understanding of what your brand represents. Start by defining your brand's mission, vision, and values. What is the purpose of your business? What do you want to achieve? What values do you want to uphold? These questions will help you shape the foundation of your brand identity.

2.4.2 Understanding Your Target Audience

TO ESTABLISH A STRONG brand identity, you need to have a deep understanding of your target audience. Who are they? What are their needs, desires, and pain points? Conduct market research and gather insights to create buyer personas that represent your ideal customers. This will help you tailor your brand messaging and visual elements to resonate with your target audience.

2.4.3 Crafting Your Brand Story

EVERY SUCCESSFUL BRAND has a compelling story behind it. Your brand story is what connects your audience to your business on an emotional level. It should communicate your brand's values, mission, and unique selling proposition. Craft a narrative that resonates with your target audience and showcases the authenticity and passion behind your business. Your brand story should be consistent across all your marketing channels and touchpoints.

2.4.4 Designing Your Visual Identity

VISUAL ELEMENTS PLAY a crucial role in establishing your brand identity. Your logo, color palette, typography, and overall design aesthetic should reflect your brand's personality and values. Invest in professional graphic design to create a visually appealing and cohesive brand identity. Consistency is key; ensure that your visual identity is consistent across your website, social media profiles, marketing materials, and any other touchpoints with your audience.

2.4.5 Crafting Your Brand Voice

YOUR BRAND VOICE IS the tone and style of communication you use to engage with your audience. It should align with your brand's personality and values. Are you formal or casual? Serious or playful? Authoritative or friendly? Define your brand voice and use it consistently in all your written content, including website copy, social media posts, emails, and blog articles. Your brand voice should resonate with your target audience and help build a strong connection with them.

2.4.6 Building a Consistent Online Presence

CONSISTENCY IS KEY when it comes to establishing your brand identity. Your online presence should be consistent across all platforms and touchpoints. Use your brand's visual elements, messaging, and tone of voice consistently in your website, social media profiles, email marketing, and any other online channels you utilize. This consistency will help reinforce your brand identity and make it easily recognizable to your audience.

2.4.7 Engaging with Your Audience

ESTABLISHING YOUR BRAND identity is not just about creating a visual identity and messaging; it's also about building relationships with your audience. Engage with your audience through social media, blog comments, email newsletters, and other channels. Respond to their comments and messages, provide valuable content, and show genuine interest in their needs and feedback. By actively engaging with your audience, you can strengthen your brand identity and build a loyal community around your business.

2.4.8 Evolving Your Brand Identity

AS YOUR BUSINESS GROWS and evolves, your brand identity may need to adapt as well. Stay attuned to market trends, customer feedback, and changes in your industry. Regularly evaluate and refine your brand identity to ensure it remains relevant and resonates with your target audience. However, be cautious not to make drastic changes that may confuse or alienate your existing customers. Evolution should be a gradual and thoughtful process.

2.4.9 Protecting Your Brand

ONCE YOU HAVE ESTABLISHED your brand identity, it is essential to protect it. Register your trademarks and copyrights to safeguard your brand's assets. Monitor your online presence and address any instances of brand infringement or misuse promptly. Building a strong brand identity takes time and effort, so it's crucial to protect it from any potential threats.

Establishing your brand identity is a continuous process that requires careful planning, creativity, and consistency. By defining your brand, understanding your target audience, crafting a compelling brand story, designing a visual identity, and engaging with your audience, you can create a strong and memorable brand presence in the digital jungle. Remember, your brand identity is not just about aesthetics; it's about building trust, loyalty, and a lasting connection with your audience.

Mastering Time and Productivity

3.1 Managing Your Time Effectively

Time management is a crucial skill for any home-based entrepreneur. With the freedom and flexibility that come with running a business from home, it can be easy to fall into the trap of procrastination or get overwhelmed by the multitude of tasks at hand. However, by implementing effective time management strategies, you can maximize your productivity, achieve your goals, and maintain a healthy work-life balance.

3.1.1 Prioritizing Your Tasks

ONE OF THE FIRST STEPS in managing your time effectively is to prioritize your tasks. Start by creating a to-do list that outlines all the tasks you need to accomplish. Then, categorize them based on their urgency and importance. This will help you identify which tasks require immediate attention and which can be tackled later.

To prioritize effectively, consider using the Eisenhower matrix. This matrix categorizes tasks into four quadrants:

1. **Urgent and Important**: These are tasks that require immediate attention and should be your top priority. They are typically deadline-driven or have significant consequences if not completed.

2. **Important but Not Urgent**: These tasks are important for your long-term goals but do not require immediate attention. Allocate dedicated time to work on these tasks to prevent them from becoming urgent.

3. **Urgent but Not Important**: These tasks may seem urgent, but they do not contribute significantly to your goals. Delegate or eliminate these tasks whenever possible to free up time for more important activities.

4. **Not Urgent and Not Important**: These tasks are time-wasters and should be avoided or minimized. They provide little value and can distract you from more meaningful work.

By categorizing your tasks using the Eisenhower Matrix, you can focus your time and energy on the most important and impactful activities.

3.1.2 Creating a Schedule

ONCE YOU HAVE PRIORITIZED your tasks, it's essential to create a schedule that allows you to allocate time for each task. Start by identifying your most productive hours of the day and blocking them off for your most critical tasks. This is when you have the highest energy and concentration levels, enabling you to tackle complex or demanding tasks more efficiently.

Consider using time-blocking techniques to allocate specific time slots for different types of activities. For example, you can dedicate the mornings to focused work, the afternoons to meetings and collaborations, and the evenings to administrative tasks or personal activities. By creating a structured schedule, you can ensure that each task receives the attention it deserves and avoid wasting time on unproductive activities.

Remember to include breaks in your schedule as well. Taking short breaks between tasks can help refresh your mind and prevent burnout. Use this time to stretch, meditate, or engage in activities that help you relax and recharge.

3.1.3 Avoiding Multitasking

WHILE MULTITASKING may seem like an efficient way to get more done in less time, it often leads to decreased productivity and increased errors. Instead of trying to juggle multiple tasks simultaneously, focus on one task at a time. This allows you to give your full attention and effort to each task, resulting in better-quality work and faster completion times.

To avoid the temptation of multitasking, practice the art of single-tasking. Set aside distractions such as email notifications or social media alerts and commit to working on one task until completion. You can also use productivity tools and apps that block distracting websites or limit your access to certain applications during designated work periods.

3.1.4 Delegating and Outsourcing

AS A HOME-BASED ENTREPRENEUR, it's important to recognize that you can't do everything on your own. Delegating and outsourcing tasks that are not within your expertise or are time-consuming can free up valuable time for more critical activities.

Identify tasks that can be delegated to others, whether it's hiring a virtual assistant, collaborating with freelancers, or outsourcing specific functions of your business. By leveraging the skills and expertise of others, you can focus on the core aspects of your business that require your attention and expertise.

3.1.5 Utilizing Time-Saving Tools and Technology

IN TODAY'S DIGITAL age, there are numerous tools and technologies available to help streamline your workflow and save time. Take advantage of project management tools, productivity apps, and automation software to automate repetitive tasks, track your progress, and stay organized.

For example, project management tools like Trello or Asana can help you create task lists, assign deadlines, and collaborate with team members. Productivity apps like Evernote or Todoist can help you capture ideas, set reminders, and manage your to-do lists. Automation tools like Zapier or IFTTT can automate repetitive tasks by connecting different apps and services.

By incorporating these time-saving tools and technologies into your workflow, you can optimize your productivity and focus on high-value activities that drive your business forward.

3.1.6 Reviewing and Adjusting Your Time Management Strategies

TIME MANAGEMENT IS not a one-size-fits-all approach. It's important to regularly review and adjust your time management strategies based on your evolving needs and circumstances. As your business grows, your priorities may shift, and new challenges may arise.

Take time to reflect on your current time management practices and identify areas for improvement. Are there any tasks that can be eliminated or delegated? Are there any time-wasting activities that can be minimized? Continuously seek ways to optimize your time and make adjustments as needed to ensure maximum productivity and efficiency.

Remember, effective time management is not about working harder but working smarter. By managing your time effectively, you can achieve a harmonious balance between your personal and professional lives while driving the success of your home-based business.

3.2 Setting Priorities and Deadlines

SETTING PRIORITIES and deadlines is crucial for achieving success in any endeavor, and running a home-based business is no exception. As a home-based entrepreneur, you have the freedom to set your own schedule and work at your own pace. However, without clear priorities and deadlines, it's easy to get overwhelmed and lose focus. In this section, we will explore the importance of setting priorities and deadlines and provide practical tips on how to effectively manage your time and stay on track.

The Power of Prioritization

SETTING PRIORITIES is all about determining what tasks or activities are most important and need to be completed first. It allows you to focus your time and energy on the activities that will have the greatest impact on your business. Without clear priorities, you may find yourself spending too much time on less important tasks, which can hinder your progress and productivity.

To effectively set priorities, start by identifying your goals and objectives. What are the key outcomes you want to achieve in your business? Once you have a clear understanding of your goals, break them down into smaller, actionable tasks. This will help you determine which tasks are most important and need to be prioritized.

One popular method for setting priorities is the Eisenhower Matrix, also known as the Urgent-Important Matrix. This matrix categorizes tasks into four quadrants based on their urgency and importance:

1. **Urgent and Important**: These are tasks that require immediate attention and have a significant impact on your business. They should be your top priority and should be completed as soon as possible.
2. **Important but Not Urgent**: These tasks are important for long-term success but do not require

immediate attention. They should be scheduled and given dedicated time slots to ensure they are completed.

3. **Urgent but Not Important**: These tasks may seem urgent, but they do not contribute significantly to your business's overall success. Delegate or eliminate these tasks whenever possible to free up time for more important activities.

4. **Not Urgent and Not Important**: These tasks are of low priority and should be avoided or minimized. They often include time-wasting activities that do not contribute to your business's growth.

By using the Eisenhower matrix, you can prioritize your tasks effectively and ensure that you are focusing on the activities that will drive your business forward.

Setting realistic deadlines

ONCE YOU HAVE SET YOUR priorities, it's essential to establish realistic deadlines for each task. Deadlines create a sense of urgency and help you stay motivated and focused. Without deadlines, tasks can easily drag on, leading to procrastination and a lack of progress.

When setting deadlines, it's important to be realistic and consider factors such as the complexity of the task, your available resources, and any external dependencies. Avoid setting overly ambitious deadlines that are impossible to meet, as this can lead to frustration and burnout.

To set realistic deadlines, break down larger tasks into smaller, manageable subtasks. Estimate the time required for each subtask and allocate sufficient time for unexpected delays or challenges. It's also helpful to build in some buffer time to account for unforeseen circumstances.

Additionally, consider your own working style and productivity patterns. Some people work best under pressure and thrive on tight deadlines, while others prefer a more relaxed pace. Find a balance that works for you and allows you to work efficiently without feeling overwhelmed.

Effective time management techniques

IN ADDITION TO SETTING priorities and deadlines, there are several time management techniques that can help you stay organized and productive:

1. **Pomodoro Technique**: This technique involves breaking your work into 25-minute intervals, called "pomodoros," followed by short breaks. It helps improve focus and productivity by working in short bursts.
2. **Time Blocking**: Time blocking involves scheduling specific blocks of time for different tasks or activities. By dedicating specific time slots to specific tasks, you can minimize distractions and ensure that each task receives the necessary attention.
3. **Batching**: Batching involves grouping similar tasks together and completing them in one go. For example, you can dedicate a specific time slot for responding to emails or making phone calls. Batching helps reduce context switching and improves efficiency.

4. **Prioritization Techniques**: In addition to the Eisenhower Matrix, there are several other prioritization techniques you can use, such as the ABC method (assigning tasks as A, B, or C based on their importance) or the 80/20 rule (focusing on the 20% of tasks that yield 80% of the results).

5. **Task Management Tools**: Utilize task management tools and apps to help you stay organized and track your progress. These tools can help you create to-do lists, set reminders, and manage deadlines effectively.

Flexibility and adaptability

WHILE SETTING PRIORITIES and deadlines is important, it's also crucial to remain flexible and adaptable. As a home-based entrepreneur, you may encounter unexpected challenges or opportunities that require adjustments to your plans. It's important to be open to change and willing to reassess your priorities and deadlines when necessary.

Regularly review and evaluate your priorities to ensure they align with your business goals. Be willing to reprioritize tasks based on changing circumstances or new information. Remember that flexibility and adaptability are key traits of successful entrepreneurs.

By setting priorities and deadlines, you can effectively manage your time, stay focused, and make progress towards your business goals. Remember to be realistic with your deadlines, utilize time management techniques, and remain flexible in your approach. With these strategies in place, you'll be well-equipped to navigate the digital jungle and achieve home-based success.

3.3 Eliminating Distractions

IN TODAY'S DIGITAL age, distractions are everywhere. From social media notifications to endless emails, it can be challenging to stay focused and productive when working from home. However, eliminating distractions is crucial if you want to achieve success in your home-based business. In this section, we will explore various strategies and techniques to help you minimize distractions and create a harmonious work environment.

3.3.1 Create a Dedicated Workspace

ONE OF THE MOST EFFECTIVE ways to eliminate distractions is to create a dedicated workspace in your home. This space should be separate from your living area and free from any potential distractions. Whether it's a spare room, a corner of your bedroom, or a home office, having a designated area solely for work can help you mentally switch into work mode and minimize interruptions.

Ensure that your workspace is organized and clutter-free. A clean and tidy environment can help you stay focused and reduce the temptation to engage in non-work-related activities. Remove any unnecessary items or distractions from your workspace, such as personal belongings or entertainment devices.

3.3.2 Establish clear boundaries.

WHEN WORKING FROM HOME, it's essential to establish clear boundaries with your family members, roommates, or anyone else sharing your living space.

Communicate your work schedule and let them know when you need uninterrupted time to focus on your business. Setting boundaries will help minimize interruptions and create a more productive work environment.

If you have children, consider establishing specific rules and routines to ensure they understand when it's appropriate to approach you during work hours. This may involve setting up designated play areas or arranging for childcare during your most critical work periods.

3.3.3 Manage Your Digital Notifications

DIGITAL NOTIFICATIONS can be a significant source of distraction. Constantly checking your email, social media, or instant messaging platforms can disrupt your workflow and decrease productivity. To eliminate distractions caused by notifications, consider implementing the following strategies:

- **Turn off non-essential notifications:** Disable notifications for non-work-related apps and platforms during your designated work hours. This includes social media, news apps, and personal email accounts. By doing so, you can minimize the temptation to check these platforms and stay focused on your business tasks.

- **Use notification management tools.** Many devices and applications offer features that allow you to customize and manage notifications. Take advantage of these tools to prioritize essential notifications and mute or silence non-essential ones.

- **Schedule dedicated time for checking notifications:** Instead of constantly interrupting your work to check notifications, schedule specific times throughout the day to review and respond to emails, messages, and social media updates. By batching these tasks, you can stay focused on your work for longer periods of time.

3.3.4 Implement time-blocking techniques

TIME BLOCKING IS A productivity technique that involves scheduling specific blocks of time for different tasks or activities. By allocating dedicated time slots for focused work, meetings, breaks, and personal activities, you can eliminate distractions and create a more structured workday.

To implement time blocking effectively, follow these steps:

1. **Identify your most productive hours.** Determine when you are most alert and focused during the day. This is the time when you should schedule your most critical and demanding tasks.
2. **Break down your tasks:** Divide your work into smaller, more manageable tasks. Assign specific time blocks for each task, ensuring that you allocate enough time to complete them without rushing or feeling overwhelmed.
3. **Eliminate multitasking:** Avoid trying to work on multiple tasks simultaneously. Instead, focus on one task at a time during each time block. This will help you maintain concentration and reduce the likelihood of getting distracted.

4. **Include breaks and downtime.** It's essential to schedule regular breaks and downtime to recharge and prevent burnout. Use these periods to relax, stretch, or engage in activities that help you clear your mind.

By implementing time-blocking techniques, you can create a structured schedule that minimizes distractions and maximizes productivity.

3.3.5 Use productivity apps and tools.

TECHNOLOGY CAN BE BOTH a source of distraction and a solution to eliminate distractions. There are numerous productivity apps and tools available that can help you stay focused and minimize interruptions. Consider incorporating the following into your workflow:

• **Focus apps:** These apps block access to distracting websites or apps for a specified period, allowing you to concentrate on your work without temptation.

• **Task management apps:** Use task management apps to organize and prioritize your work. These tools can help you stay on track and ensure that you complete your tasks efficiently.

• **Time tracking apps:** Time tracking apps can help you monitor how you spend your time and identify areas where you may be getting distracted. By analyzing your time usage, you can make adjustments to improve your productivity.

• **Noise-cancelling headphones:** If you work in a noisy environment, consider investing in noise-cancelling headphones. These can help block out external distractions and create a more focused work atmosphere.

3.3.6 Practice mindfulness and meditation.

DISTRACTIONS OFTEN arise from within our own minds. To combat internal distractions, practicing mindfulness and meditation can be highly beneficial. These practices help cultivate focus, reduce stress, and improve overall mental well-being.

Consider incorporating short mindfulness or meditation sessions into your daily routine. Set aside a few minutes each day to sit quietly, focus on your breath, and observe your thoughts without judgment. This practice can help train your mind to stay present and minimize distractions.

3.3.7 Seek Accountability and Support

SOMETIMES, ELIMINATING distractions requires external support. Find an accountability partner or join a mastermind group of like-minded individuals who are also working from home. By sharing your goals, challenges, and progress with others, you can gain valuable insights and support to stay on track.

Additionally, consider seeking professional help or guidance if you find it challenging to eliminate distractions on your own. A business coach or productivity expert can provide personalized strategies and techniques to help you overcome distractions and achieve your goals.

By implementing these strategies and techniques, you can create a focused and distraction-free work environment, leading to increased productivity and success in your home-based business. Remember, eliminating distractions is an ongoing process that requires discipline and commitment. Stay mindful of your work habits, and continuously evaluate and adjust your strategies to maintain harmony in the digital jungle.

3.4 Boosting Productivity with Technology

IN TODAY'S DIGITAL age, technology has become an integral part of our lives, both personally and professionally. For home-based entrepreneurs, leveraging technology can be a game-changer when it comes to boosting productivity and achieving success. From streamlining tasks to automating processes, technology offers a wide range of tools and solutions that can help you work smarter, not harder. In this section, we will explore some of the key ways you can harness the power of technology to enhance your productivity and take your home-based business to new heights.

3.4.1 Embracing Project Management Tools

ONE OF THE BIGGEST challenges for home-based entrepreneurs is managing multiple projects and tasks simultaneously. This is where project management tools come in handy. These tools provide a centralized platform where you can organize and track all your projects, tasks, and deadlines. With features like task assignments, progress tracking, and deadline reminders, project management tools help you stay on top of your workload and ensure that nothing falls through the cracks.

Popular project management tools like Trello, Asana, and Monday.com offer intuitive interfaces and customizable workflows that cater to different business needs. By utilizing these tools, you can create a visual representation of your projects, set priorities, and allocate resources efficiently. This not only enhances your productivity but also improves collaboration and communication with team members, if applicable.

3.4.2 Automating Repetitive Tasks

AS A HOME-BASED ENTREPRENEUR, you often find yourself juggling various repetitive tasks that consume a significant amount of your time and energy. This is where automation comes to the rescue. By automating repetitive tasks, you can free up valuable time to focus on more important aspects of your business.

There are numerous automation tools available that can help you streamline your workflow. For example, email marketing platforms like Mailchimp and ConvertKit allow you to automate email campaigns, saving you the hassle of manually sending individual emails. Social media scheduling tools like Hootsuite and Buffer enable you to schedule posts in advance, ensuring a consistent online presence without the need for constant manual updates.

Additionally, you can explore automation tools like Zapier and IFTTT, which allow you to connect different apps and services to create automated workflows. For instance, you can set up a workflow that automatically saves email attachments to cloud storage or sends you a notification when a new lead is generated on your website. By automating these tasks, you can eliminate the need for manual intervention and focus on more strategic aspects of your business.

3.4.3 Leveraging Communication and Collaboration Tools

EFFECTIVE COMMUNICATION and collaboration are crucial for the success of any business, regardless of its size or location. As a home-based entrepreneur, you need to stay connected with clients, team members, and other stakeholders to ensure smooth operations. Technology offers a plethora of communication and collaboration tools that can bridge the gap and facilitate seamless interactions.

Instant messaging platforms like Slack and Microsoft Teams allow you to communicate with team members in real-time, regardless of their physical location. These tools offer features like group chats, file sharing, and video conferencing, enabling you to collaborate effectively and stay connected with your team.

Video conferencing tools like Zoom and Google Meet have gained immense popularity, especially in the wake of remote work becoming the new norm. These tools allow you to conduct virtual meetings, presentations, and training sessions, eliminating the need for physical presence and saving time and resources.

Cloud-based document collaboration tools like Google Docs and Microsoft Office 365 enable multiple users to work on the same document simultaneously, making it easy to collaborate on projects and share feedback in real-time. These tools also offer version control and automatic saving, ensuring that you never lose your work.

3.4.4 Harnessing the Power of Productivity Apps

IN ADDITION TO PROJECT management, automation, and communication tools, there are a wide range of productivity apps available that can help you stay organized, focused, and efficient. These apps are designed to enhance your productivity by providing features like task management, time tracking, note-taking, and goal setting.

Task management apps like Todoist, Wunderlist, and Any.do help you create to-do lists, set reminders, and prioritize tasks. These apps ensure that you stay on top of your daily responsibilities and never miss a deadline.

Time-tracking apps like Toggl and RescueTime help you monitor how you spend your time, identify time-wasting activities, and optimize your workflow accordingly. By gaining insights into your time usage, you can make informed decisions about how to allocate your time more effectively.

Note-taking apps like Evernote and OneNote allow you to capture ideas, create checklists, and organize information in a digital format. These apps make it easy to access and retrieve information whenever you need it, eliminating the need for physical notebooks and sticky notes.

Goal-setting apps like Habitica and Strides help you set goals, track progress, and stay motivated. These apps provide a visual representation of your goals and offer reminders and rewards to keep you on track.

By incorporating these productivity apps into your daily routine, you can optimize your workflow, stay organized, and maximize your productivity.

3.4.5 Ensuring Data Security and Backup

AS A HOME-BASED ENTREPRENEUR, your business data is one of your most valuable assets. It is essential to prioritize data security and backup to protect your business from potential threats like data breaches, hardware failures, or natural disasters.

Cloud storage services like Google Drive, Dropbox, and OneDrive offer secure and reliable storage solutions for your business data. These services allow you to store and access your files from anywhere, ensuring that your data is safe and accessible even in the event of a hardware failure or loss.

Implementing robust cybersecurity measures like strong passwords, two-factor authentication, and regular software updates is crucial to safeguarding your business data from unauthorized access. Additionally, investing in antivirus software and firewalls can provide an extra layer of protection against malware and cyber threats.

Regularly backing up your data is essential to ensuring that you can recover your files in case of any unforeseen circumstances. Cloud backup services like Backblaze and Carbonite automatically back up your files to the cloud, providing an additional layer of protection against data loss.

By prioritizing data security and backup, you can have peace of mind knowing that your business data is safe and protected.

In conclusion, technology offers a plethora of tools and solutions that can significantly enhance your productivity as a home-based entrepreneur. By embracing project management tools, automating repetitive tasks, leveraging communication and collaboration tools, harnessing the power of productivity apps, and ensuring data security and backup, you can streamline your workflow, optimize your time, and achieve greater success in your home-based business. Embrace the power of technology and unlock your full potential in the digital jungle.

3.5 Maintaining Work-Life Balance

MAINTAINING A HEALTHY work-life balance is crucial for the success and well-being of any home-based entrepreneur. In the digital age, where work can easily spill over into personal life, it is essential to establish boundaries and find harmony between your professional and personal responsibilities. This section will explore strategies and tips to help you maintain a healthy work-life balance while running a successful home-based business.

3.5.1 Setting Boundaries

ONE OF THE FIRST STEPS in maintaining work-life balance is setting clear boundaries between your work and personal life. When working from home, it can be tempting to blur the lines between the two, leading to burnout and decreased productivity. Here are some strategies to help you establish boundaries:

1. **Designate a workspace**: Create a dedicated workspace in your home where you can focus on your work. This will help you mentally separate your work life from your personal life.
2. **Set specific working hours.** Establish a schedule and

stick to it. Determine the hours during which you will be working and communicate them to your clients, colleagues, and family members. This will help you create a routine and manage expectations.

3. **Turn off notifications**: Avoid the constant distractions of emails, messages, and social media notifications by setting specific times to check and respond to them. This will allow you to focus on your work without interruptions.

4. **Communicate with your family**: If you have family members at home, communicate with them about your working hours and the importance of uninterrupted time. This will help them understand when you need to concentrate and minimize distractions.

3.5.2 Prioritizing Self-Care

TAKING CARE OF YOURSELF is essential for maintaining work-life balance. When you prioritize self-care, you are better equipped to handle the demands of your business and personal life. Here are some self-care strategies to consider:

1. **Schedule breaks**: Incorporate regular breaks into your workday to recharge and relax. Use this time to engage in activities that bring you joy and help you unwind, such as going for a walk, practicing mindfulness, or reading a book.

2. **Exercise regularly.** Physical activity is not only beneficial for your health but also for your mental well-being. Find an exercise routine that works for

you, whether it's going to the gym, practicing yoga, or taking a dance class. Regular exercise can boost your energy levels and reduce stress.

3. **Practice stress management techniques**: Find stress management techniques that work for you, such as deep breathing exercises, meditation, or journaling. These practices can help you alleviate stress and maintain a calm and focused mindset.

4. **Maintain a healthy lifestyle**: Ensure you are getting enough sleep, eating nutritious meals, and staying hydrated. A healthy lifestyle will provide you with the energy and vitality needed to manage both your work and personal life effectively.

3.5.3 Time Management Strategies

EFFECTIVE TIME MANAGEMENT is key to maintaining a work-life balance. By managing your time efficiently, you can accomplish your work tasks while still having time for personal activities. Consider the following time-management strategies:

1. **Create a schedule.** Plan your day in advance by creating a schedule that includes both work-related tasks and personal activities. This will help you stay organized and ensure that you allocate time for both aspects of your life.

2. **Set realistic goals**: Set achievable goals for each day or week. Break down larger tasks into smaller, manageable ones to avoid feeling overwhelmed. Celebrate your accomplishments as you complete each task, which will motivate you to stay on track.

3. **Delegate and outsource**: Identify tasks that can be delegated or outsourced to others. This could include hiring a virtual assistant, outsourcing certain business functions, or asking for help from family members. Delegating tasks will free up your time and allow you to focus on more important aspects of your business and personal life.

4. **Practice the Pomodoro Technique**: The Pomodoro Technique is a time management method that involves working in focused bursts of time, typically 25 minutes, followed by a short break. This technique can help improve your productivity and prevent burnout.

3.5.4 Nurture Relationships

MAINTAINING WORK-LIFE balance also involves nurturing relationships with your loved ones and building a support network. Here are some strategies to help you foster meaningful connections:

1. **Schedule quality time.** Set aside dedicated time to spend with your family and friends. This could be a weekly family dinner, a date night with your partner, or a catch-up session with friends. By scheduling quality time, you can ensure that you prioritize your relationships.

2. **Join networking groups**: Engage with like-minded entrepreneurs by joining networking groups or online communities. These platforms provide opportunities to connect with others who

understand the challenges of running a home-based business and can offer support and advice.

3. **Find a mentor or coach.** Seek guidance from experienced entrepreneurs who can provide valuable insights and help you navigate the ups and downs of running a business. A mentor or coach can offer advice on work-life balance and share strategies for success.

4. **Practice active listening.** When spending time with loved ones, practice active listening. Show genuine interest in their lives, thoughts, and feelings. This will strengthen your relationships and create a sense of connection and support.

Maintaining work-life balance is an ongoing process that requires conscious effort and regular evaluation. By setting boundaries, prioritizing self-care, managing your time effectively, and nurturing relationships, you can achieve harmony in the digital jungle and create a successful home-based business while enjoying a fulfilling personal life.

3.6 Overcoming Procrastination

PROCRASTINATION IS a common challenge that many individuals face, regardless of whether they work from home or in a traditional office setting. It is the act of delaying or postponing tasks, often resulting in decreased productivity and increased stress levels. In the context of a home-based business, overcoming procrastination is crucial for achieving success and maintaining a harmonious work-life balance. In this section, we will explore various strategies and techniques to help you overcome procrastination and stay focused on your goals.

3.6.1 Understanding the Root Causes of Procrastination

BEFORE WE DELVE INTO the strategies to overcome procrastination, it is important to understand the underlying reasons why we procrastinate. By identifying the root causes, we can develop targeted solutions to address them effectively. Some common causes of procrastination include the following:

Fear of Failure

ONE OF THE PRIMARY reasons people procrastinate is the fear of failure. When faced with a challenging task or project, the fear of not meeting expectations or making mistakes can be paralyzing. As a result, individuals may choose to delay starting the task altogether.

Lack of clarity

ANOTHER COMMON CAUSE of procrastination is a lack of clarity about the task at hand. When we are unsure about the steps involved or the desired outcome, it can be difficult to take the first step. This uncertainty can lead to procrastination as we try to avoid making mistakes or taking the wrong approach.

Overwhelm

FEELING OVERWHELMED by the sheer volume of tasks or the complexity of a project can also contribute to procrastination. When we perceive a task as too big or too challenging, we may feel overwhelmed and choose to delay starting it.

Perfectionism

PERFECTIONISM IS ANOTHER factor that often leads to procrastination. When we set unrealistically high standards for ourselves, we may fear that our work will not meet those standards. This fear of falling short can prevent us from starting or completing tasks.

3.6.2 Strategies to Overcome Procrastination

NOW THAT WE HAVE IDENTIFIED some common causes of procrastination, let's explore strategies to overcome this challenge and enhance your productivity:

Set clear goals and priorities.

START BY SETTING CLEAR goals and priorities for your home-based business. When you have a clear vision of what you want to achieve, it becomes easier to prioritize tasks and stay focused. Break down larger goals into smaller, manageable tasks, and assign deadlines to each task. This will help you stay organized and motivated.

Create a schedule and stick to it.

DEVELOPING A SCHEDULE and sticking to it is essential for overcoming procrastination. Set aside specific blocks of time for different tasks and activities, and commit to following your schedule. Treat these time blocks as non-negotiable appointments with yourself, and avoid distractions during these periods.

Use time management techniques.

UTILIZE TIME MANAGEMENT techniques such as the Pomodoro Technique or time blocking to enhance your productivity. The Pomodoro Technique involves working in focused bursts of 25 minutes, followed by a short break. This technique can help you maintain focus and avoid burnout. Time blocking involves allocating specific time slots for different tasks, ensuring that you dedicate uninterrupted time to each task.

Break tasks into smaller steps.

IF A TASK FEELS OVERWHELMING, break it down into smaller, more manageable steps. By focusing on one step at a time, you can reduce feelings of overwhelm and make progress towards completing the task. Celebrate each small accomplishment, as it will provide motivation to continue working.

Practice Self-Compassion

BE KIND TO YOURSELF and practice self-compassion. Acknowledge that everyone experiences procrastination at times, and it does not define your abilities or worth. Instead of berating yourself for procrastinating, focus on finding solutions and taking positive action.

Find an accountability partner.

HAVING AN ACCOUNTABILITY partner can be highly effective in overcoming procrastination. Find someone who shares similar goals or works in a similar field, and hold each other accountable for completing tasks. Regular check-ins and sharing progress can provide motivation and support.

Minimize Distractions

IDENTIFY AND MINIMIZE distractions in your work environment. Turn off notifications on your phone, close unnecessary tabs on your computer, and create a dedicated workspace that is free from distractions. Consider using productivity apps or browser extensions that block access to distracting websites during work hours.

Practice mindfulness and visualization.

INCORPORATE MINDFULNESS and visualization techniques into your daily routine. Mindfulness can help you stay present and focused on the task at hand, reducing the tendency to procrastinate. Visualization involves mentally picturing yourself successfully completing a task or project, which can increase motivation and drive.

Reward Yourself

CREATE A SYSTEM OF rewards for completing tasks or reaching milestones. Treat yourself to something you enjoy after completing a challenging task or meeting a deadline. These rewards can serve as positive reinforcement and help combat procrastination.

3.6.3 Developing a Procrastination-Busting Mindset

OVERCOMING PROCRASTINATION requires a shift in mindset. Here are some key principles to adopt:

Embrace Imperfection

ACCEPT THAT PERFECTION is not attainable and that mistakes are a natural part of the learning process. Embrace imperfection and focus on progress rather than perfection.

Cultivate Self-Discipline

DEVELOP SELF-DISCIPLINE by consistently practicing the strategies mentioned earlier. It takes time and effort to overcome procrastination, but with consistent practice, you can develop the discipline needed to stay focused and productive.

Stay Motivated

FIND WAYS TO STAY MOTIVATED and inspired. Surround yourself with positive influences, read books or listen to podcasts that inspire you, and regularly revisit your goals to remind yourself of the bigger picture.

Learn from setbacks.

VIEW SETBACKS AND FAILURES as opportunities for growth and learning. Instead of dwelling on past mistakes, analyze what went wrong and use that knowledge to improve your approach in the future.

Celebrate Progress

CELEBRATE YOUR PROGRESS and achievements along the way. Recognize and appreciate the effort you put into overcoming procrastination and achieving your goals.

By implementing these strategies and adopting a proactive mindset, you can overcome procrastination and unlock your full potential in your home-based business. Remember, overcoming procrastination is a journey, and it requires consistent effort and self-reflection. Stay committed to your goals, and you will reap the rewards of increased productivity and success.

Marketing and Promotion Strategies

4.1 Understanding Your Target Audience

In order to effectively market and promote your home-based business, it is crucial to have a deep understanding of your target audience. Your target audience consists of a specific group of people who are most likely to be interested in your products or services. By understanding their needs, preferences, and behaviors, you can tailor your marketing strategies to effectively reach and engage with them. In this section, we will explore the importance of understanding your target audience and provide you with practical tips on how to gain valuable insights about them.

4.1.1 Defining Your Target Audience

BEFORE YOU CAN UNDERSTAND your target audience, you need to clearly define who they are. Start by identifying the demographics of your potential customers, such as age, gender, location, and income level. This will help you create a general profile of your target audience. However, demographics alone are not enough to fully understand your audience. You also need to consider their psychographics, which include their interests, values, attitudes, and lifestyle choices. By combining both demographics and psychographics, you can create a more comprehensive picture of your target audience.

4.1.2 Conducting Market Research

MARKET RESEARCH IS a valuable tool for gaining insights about your target audience. It involves collecting and analyzing data about your industry, competitors, and customers. There are several methods you can use to conduct market research:

1. Surveys: Create online surveys or questionnaires to gather information directly from your target audience. Ask questions about their preferences, needs, and purchasing habits. You can use free online survey tools or hire a market research firm to conduct surveys on your behalf.
2. Interviews: Conduct one-on-one interviews with your existing customers or potential customers. This allows you to have in-depth conversations and gain a deeper understanding of their motivations and pain points.
3. Social Media Listening: Monitor social media platforms to see what people are saying about your industry, competitors, and products. Pay attention to their comments, reviews, and discussions to identify trends and gather insights.
4. Competitor Analysis: Study your competitors to understand their target audience and marketing strategies. Look at their websites, social media

profiles, and customer reviews to identify gaps and opportunities in the market.

5. Analytics Tools: Utilize web analytics tools to gather data about your website visitors. Analyze metrics such as demographics, behavior flow, and conversion rates to gain insights about your target audience.

4.1.3 Creating Buyer Personas

ONCE YOU HAVE GATHERED data and insights about your target audience, you can create buyer personas. A buyer's persona is a fictional representation of your ideal customer. It includes details such as their demographics, psychographics, goals, challenges, and buying behaviors. Creating buyer personas helps you humanize your target audience and understand their needs and motivations on a deeper level. It also allows you to tailor your marketing messages and strategies to resonate with each persona.

To create buyer personas, start by identifying common characteristics and patterns among your target audience. Group them into segments based on their similarities. Then, give each segment a name and create a detailed profile for each persona. Include information such as their age, occupation, hobbies, goals, challenges, and preferred communication channels. The more detailed and specific your buyer personas are, the better you can target your marketing efforts.

4.1.4 Analyzing Customer Feedback

CUSTOMER FEEDBACK IS a valuable source of information about your target audience. It provides insights into their satisfaction levels, preferences, and areas for improvement. There are several ways to collect customer feedback:

1. Surveys: Send post-purchase surveys or feedback forms to gather feedback from your customers. Ask them about their experience with your products or services, what they liked or disliked, and any suggestions they may have.
2. Reviews and Testimonials: Monitor online review platforms and social media for customer reviews and testimonials. Pay attention to both positive and negative feedback to identify areas for improvement and areas where you excel.
3. Customer Support Interactions: Analyze customer support interactions, such as emails or live chats, to identify common questions, concerns, and pain points. This can help you address customer needs more effectively.
4. Social Media Listening: Monitor social media platforms for mentions of your brand or products. Engage with customers who mention you and address any issues or concerns they may have.

By analyzing customer feedback, you can gain valuable insights into the needs and preferences of your target audience. Use this information to improve your products or services and tailor your marketing messages to better resonate with your customers.

4.1.5 Staying Up-to-Date with Market Trends

UNDERSTANDING YOUR target audience is an ongoing process. Market trends and consumer preferences can change rapidly, so it is important to stay up-to-date with the latest developments in your industry. Keep an eye on industry publications, blogs, and news outlets to stay informed about emerging trends, technologies, and consumer behaviors. Attend industry conferences and events to network with other professionals and gain insights from industry experts. By staying informed and adapting to changes in the market, you can ensure that your marketing strategies remain relevant and effective.

In conclusion, understanding your target audience is essential for the success of your home-based business. By defining your target audience, conducting market research, creating buyer personas, analyzing customer feedback, and staying up-to-date with market trends, you can gain valuable insights that will inform your marketing strategies and help you effectively reach and engage with your target audience. Remember, the more you understand your audience, the better you can meet their needs and build long-lasting relationships with them.

4.2 Creating a Marketing Plan

IN TODAY'S DIGITAL age, having a well-defined marketing plan is crucial for the success of any home-based business. A marketing plan serves as a roadmap that outlines the strategies and tactics you will use to promote your products or services, attract customers, and ultimately achieve your business goals.

By creating a comprehensive marketing plan, you can effectively reach your target audience, build brand awareness, and drive sales. In this section, we will explore the key components of a marketing plan and provide you with practical tips to create a plan that aligns with your home-based business.

4.2.1 Defining Your Marketing Objectives

BEFORE DIVING INTO the specifics of your marketing plan, it is essential to define your marketing objectives. What do you hope to achieve through your marketing efforts? Are you looking to increase brand awareness, generate leads, drive website traffic, or boost sales? By clearly defining your marketing objectives, you can tailor your strategies and tactics to meet these goals. It is important to set realistic and measurable objectives that can be tracked and evaluated over time.

4.2.2 Identifying Your Target Audience

TO EFFECTIVELY MARKET your products or services, you need to have a deep understanding of your target audience. Who are your ideal customers? What are their demographics, interests, and pain points? By identifying your target audience, you can tailor your marketing messages and channels to resonate with them. Conduct market research, analyze customer data, and engage with your audience to gain insights into their needs and preferences. This information will help you create targeted and personalized marketing campaigns that are more likely to yield positive results.

4.2.3 Conducting a Competitive Analysis

TO STAND OUT IN THE digital jungle, it is crucial to understand your competition. Conducting a competitive analysis allows you to identify your competitors' strengths and weaknesses, their marketing strategies, and their unique selling propositions. By analyzing your competition, you can identify gaps in the market and find opportunities to differentiate your home-based business. Look at their online presence, social media activities, content marketing efforts, and customer reviews. This information will help you refine your marketing strategies and position your business effectively.

4.2.4 Choosing the Right Marketing Channels

IN THE DIGITAL AGE, there are numerous marketing channels available to promote your home-based business. From social media platforms to email marketing, search engine optimization (SEO), content marketing, and paid advertising, it is important to choose the channels that align with your target audience and marketing objectives. Each channel has its own strengths and weaknesses, so it is crucial to evaluate which ones will yield the best results for your business. Consider factors such as cost, reach, engagement, and conversion rates when selecting your marketing channels.

4.2.5 Crafting Compelling Marketing Messages

ONCE YOU HAVE IDENTIFIED your target audience and chosen your marketing channels, it is time to craft compelling marketing messages. Your marketing messages should clearly communicate the value and benefits of your products or services to your target audience. Use persuasive language, highlight unique selling propositions, and address your customers' pain points. Tailor your messages to resonate with different segments of your target audience and ensure consistency across all marketing channels. Compelling marketing messages will capture the attention of your audience and motivate them to take action.

4.2.6 Setting a Budget

MARKETING CAN BE A significant expense for any business, including home-based businesses. It is important to set a realistic marketing budget that aligns with your financial resources and marketing objectives. Consider the costs associated with different marketing channels, such as advertising fees, content creation, graphic design, and marketing software. Allocate your budget strategically to maximize your return on investment (ROI). Regularly review and adjust your marketing budget based on the performance of your marketing campaigns and the availability of funds.

4.2.7 Implementing and Evaluating Your Marketing Strategies

ONCE YOU HAVE DEVELOPED your marketing plan, it is time to implement your strategies and tactics. Execute your marketing campaigns across the chosen channels, monitor their performance, and make adjustments as needed. Use analytics tools to track key metrics such as website traffic, conversion rates, social media engagement, and email open rates. Regularly evaluate the effectiveness of your marketing strategies and make data-driven decisions to optimize your campaigns. Continuously test and refine your marketing efforts to improve results and achieve your marketing objectives.

4.2.8 Staying Up-to-Date with Marketing Trends

THE DIGITAL LANDSCAPE is constantly evolving, and new marketing trends emerge regularly. To stay ahead of the competition and effectively market your home-based business, it is important to stay up-to-date with the latest marketing trends and best practices. Follow industry blogs, attend webinars, and participate in online communities to learn about new strategies, tools, and technologies. Experiment with new marketing tactics and adapt your marketing plan accordingly. By staying informed and agile, you can leverage the latest marketing trends to gain a competitive edge in the digital jungle.

In conclusion, creating a marketing plan is essential for the success of your home-based business in the digital jungle. By defining your marketing objectives, identifying your target audience, conducting a competitive analysis, choosing the right marketing channels, crafting compelling marketing messages, setting a budget, implementing and evaluating your strategies, and staying up-to-date with marketing trends, you can develop a comprehensive marketing plan that drives the growth and success of your home-based business. Remember, a well-executed marketing plan is the key to unlocking the secrets of home-based success in the digital age.

4.3 Utilizing Social Media for Business Growth

IN TODAY'S DIGITAL age, social media has become an integral part of our daily lives. It has transformed the way we communicate, connect, and consume information. As a home-based business owner, harnessing the power of social media can be a game-changer for your business's growth. It provides you with a cost-effective and efficient way to reach your target audience, build brand awareness, and drive sales. In this section, we will explore the various strategies and techniques you can use to utilize social media for the growth of your home-based business.

4.3.1 Choosing the Right Social Media Platforms

WITH NUMEROUS SOCIAL media platforms available, it is essential to choose the ones that align with your business goals and target audience. Each platform has its own unique features and user demographics, so understanding your audience's preferences and behaviors is crucial. Here are some popular social media platforms and their key characteristics:

1. Facebook: With over 2.8 billion monthly active users, Facebook is the largest social media platform. It offers a wide range of features, including business pages, groups, and advertising options. It is suitable for businesses targeting a broad audience.
2. Instagram: Known for its visual content, Instagram is popular among younger demographics. It is ideal for businesses that can showcase their products or

services through high-quality images and videos.

3. Twitter: Twitter is a microblogging platform that allows users to share short messages called tweets. It is suitable for businesses that want to engage in real-time conversations and share timely updates.

4. LinkedIn: LinkedIn is a professional networking platform that caters to businesses and professionals. It is an excellent platform for B2B businesses and those looking to establish thought leadership in their industry.

5. Pinterest: Pinterest is a visual discovery platform that focuses on inspiration and ideas. It is ideal for businesses in the fashion, home decor, food, and lifestyle industries.

6. YouTube: As a video-sharing platform, YouTube is perfect for businesses that can create engaging and informative video content. It is the second-largest search engine after Google, making it an excellent platform for SEO optimization.

Remember, it is not necessary to be present on every social media platform. Focus on the platforms that align with your target audience and where you can create meaningful and engaging content.

4.3.2 Creating a Social Media Strategy

TO EFFECTIVELY UTILIZE social media for business growth, it is essential to have a well-defined strategy in place. A social media strategy outlines your goals, target audience, content plan, and metrics for success. Here are some key steps to creating a social media strategy:

1. Define your goals: Determine what you want to achieve through social media. It could be increasing brand awareness, driving website traffic, generating leads, or boosting sales.

2. Identify your target audience. Understand your target audience's demographics, interests, and online behaviors. This information will help you tailor your content and messaging to resonate with them.

3. Choose the right content mix. Decide on the types of content you will create and share on social media. It could include blog posts, videos, infographics, customer testimonials, behind-the-scenes glimpses, and more.

4. Plan your content calendar: Create a content calendar to schedule your social media posts in advance. This ensures consistency and helps you stay organized.

5. Engage with your audience: Social media is not just about broadcasting your message; it's also about building relationships. Respond to comments, messages, and mentions promptly. Engage with your audience by asking questions, running polls, and encouraging user-generated content.

6. Monitor and analyze your results. Regularly track your social media metrics to evaluate the effectiveness of your strategy. Use the analytics tools provided by each platform or third-party tools to gain insights

into your audience's engagement, reach, and conversions.

4.3.3 Engaging and Growing Your Social Media Audience

BUILDING A STRONG AND engaged social media audience is crucial for the growth of your home-based business. Here are some strategies to engage and grow your social media following:

1. Consistent posting: Regularly post high-quality content to keep your audience engaged. Aim for a consistent posting schedule that aligns with your audience's online habits.
2. Use visuals: Visual content is more likely to grab attention and drive engagement. Incorporate eye-catching images, videos, and infographics into your social media posts.
3. Encourage user-generated content: Encourage your audience to create and share content related to your brand. This could include testimonials, reviews, or creative uses of your products. User-generated content not only boosts engagement but also acts as social proof for your business.
4. Run contests and giveaways: Contests and giveaways are an effective way to increase engagement and attract new followers. Encourage participants to like, share, and tag their friends to expand your reach.
5. Collaborate with influencers: Partnering with influencers in your industry can help you reach a

wider audience and build credibility. Look for
influencers whose values align with your brand and
who collaborate on content or promotions.

6. Engage in conversations: Actively participate in
relevant conversations and discussions on social
media. This helps you establish yourself as an
authority in your industry and build relationships
with potential customers.

Remember, growing your social media audience takes time
and effort. Focus on providing value, being authentic, and
building meaningful connections with your followers.

4.3.4 Paid Advertising on Social Media

WHILE ORGANIC REACH and engagement are essential,
paid advertising on social media can significantly boost your
business's growth. Social media platforms offer various
advertising options to target specific audiences and achieve
your business goals. Here are some common types of social
media advertising:

1. Facebook Ads: Facebook offers a wide range of ad
formats, including image ads, video ads, carousel ads,
and more. You can target specific demographics,
interests, and behaviors to reach your ideal audience.

2. Instagram Ads: Instagram ads appear in users' feeds
and stories. You can create visually appealing ads that
blend seamlessly with organic content. Instagram also
offers various targeting options to reach your desired
audience.

3. LinkedIn Ads: LinkedIn ads allow you to target professionals based on their job titles, industries, and company sizes. It is an effective platform for B2B businesses looking to reach decision-makers.
4. Twitter Ads: Twitter offers promoted tweets, accounts, and trends to help you reach a wider audience. You can target users based on their interests, demographics, and keywords.
5. YouTube Ads: YouTube offers various ad formats, including skippable and non-skippable video ads, overlay ads, and sponsored cards. You can target users based on their demographics, interests, and search behavior.

When running paid social media ads, it is crucial to define your target audience, set clear objectives, and monitor your ad performance. Regularly analyze your ad metrics to optimize your campaigns and maximize your return on investment.

4.3.5 Building Relationships and Customer Loyalty

SOCIAL MEDIA IS NOT just about acquiring new customers; it is also a powerful tool for building relationships and fostering customer loyalty. Here are some strategies to strengthen your relationships with your social media audience:

1. Respond to comments and messages: Promptly respond to comments, messages, and mentions on social media. Show your audience that you value their feedback and are attentive to their needs.

2. Personalize your interactions: Address your audience by their names whenever possible. Personalize your responses and make them feel heard and appreciated.

3. Share user-generated content: Showcase user-generated content on your social media platforms. This not only acknowledges and appreciates your customers but also encourages others to engage with your brand.

4. Offer exclusive promotions and discounts: Reward your social media followers with exclusive promotions, discounts, or early access to new products or services. This creates a sense of exclusivity and encourages customer loyalty.

5. Provide valuable content: Share informative and valuable content that educates and helps your audience. This positions you as an expert in your industry and builds trust with your followers.

6. Conduct surveys and polls: Engage your audience by conducting surveys and polls to gather their opinions and preferences. This not only helps you understand your audience better but also makes them feel involved in your business.

By focusing on building relationships and fostering customer loyalty, you can turn your social media followers into brand advocates who will not only support your business but also recommend it to others.

Conclusion

SOCIAL MEDIA HAS REVOLUTIONIZED the way businesses connect with their audience and promote their products or services. By utilizing social media effectively, you can reach a wider audience, build brand awareness, and drive business growth. Remember to choose the right social media platforms, create a well-defined strategy, engage and grow your audience, consider paid advertising options, and focus on building relationships with your customers. With a thoughtful and consistent approach, social media can become a powerful tool in your home-based business's success.

4.4 Implementing Effective Email Marketing

EMAIL MARKETING IS a powerful tool that can help home-based businesses reach their target audience, build relationships, and drive sales. In this section, we will explore the strategies and best practices for implementing effective email marketing campaigns.

4.4.1 Building an Email List

BEFORE YOU CAN START implementing email marketing, you need to build a quality email list. This list will consist of individuals who have willingly provided their email addresses and have expressed interest in your products or services. Here are some effective strategies for building an email list:

1. **Opt-in Forms**: Place opt-in forms on your website, blog, and social media platforms to capture email

addresses. Offer incentives such as exclusive content, discounts, or freebies to encourage visitors to sign up.

2. **Lead Magnets**: Create valuable lead magnets such as ebooks, guides, or templates that visitors can download in exchange for their email addresses. Make sure the lead magnet is relevant to your target audience and provides genuine value.

3. **Content Upgrades**: Offer content upgrades within your blog posts or articles. These are additional resources or bonus content that readers can access by providing their email addresses.

4. **Events and Webinars**: Host webinars or events and require attendees to register with their email addresses. This not only helps you build your email list but also allows you to engage with your audience in a more personal way.

5. **Partnerships and Collaborations**: Collaborate with other businesses or influencers in your industry to cross-promote each other's email lists. This can help you reach a wider audience and attract new subscribers.

Remember, it's important to obtain permission from individuals before adding them to your email list. Implementing double opt-in, where subscribers confirm their email addresses, ensures that you have a list of engaged and interested individuals.

4.4.2 Crafting Compelling Email Content

ONCE YOU HAVE BUILT your email list, it's time to craft compelling email content that engages your subscribers and drives action. Here are some tips for creating effective email content:

1. **Personalization**: Address your subscribers by their names and segment your email list based on their interests, preferences, or purchase history. Personalized emails have higher open and click-through rates.

2. **Clear and Concise Subject Lines**: Write subject lines that grab attention and clearly convey the value or benefit of opening the email. Keep them concise, and avoid using spammy or misleading language.

3. **Compelling Copy**: Write engaging and persuasive copy that speaks directly to your subscribers' pain points and offers solutions. Use storytelling techniques, bullet points, and subheadings to make your emails easy to read and digest.

4. **Call-to-Action (CTA)**: Include a clear and prominent call-to-action in your emails. Whether it's to make a purchase, sign up for a webinar, or download a resource, make sure your CTA stands out and is easy to follow.

5. **Mobile Optimization**: With the majority of emails being opened on mobile devices, it's crucial to optimize your emails for mobile viewing. Use a responsive email template, and keep your design simple and easy to navigate.

6. **A/B Testing**: Experiment with different elements of your emails, such as subject lines, copy, CTAs, and visuals, to see what resonates best with your audience. A/B testing allows you to optimize your email campaigns for better results.

4.4.3 Automation and Segmentation

AUTOMATION AND SEGMENTATION are key to maximizing the effectiveness of your email marketing campaigns. By automating certain processes and segmenting your email list, you can deliver more targeted and personalized content to your subscribers. Here's how you can leverage automation and segmentation:

1. **Welcome Emails**: Set up automated welcome emails to greet new subscribers and introduce them to your brand. Use this opportunity to provide valuable information, set expectations, and encourage engagement.
2. **Drip Campaigns**: Create automated drip campaigns that deliver a series of emails over a specific period of time. Drip campaigns are effective for nurturing leads, onboarding new customers, or promoting a specific product or service.
3. **Behavioral Triggers**: Set up triggers based on your subscribers' actions or behaviors. For example, if a subscriber abandons their cart, you can automatically send them a reminder email with a special offer to encourage them to complete the purchase.
4. **Segmentation**: Divide your email list into segments

based on demographics, interests, purchase history, or engagement level. This allows you to send targeted emails that are more relevant to each segment, increasing the chances of conversion.

5. **Re-engagement Campaigns**: Identify subscribers who have become inactive and send them re-engagement campaigns to win them back. Offer incentives, ask for feedback, or provide exclusive content to reignite their interest.

4.4.4 Analyzing and Optimizing Email Campaigns

TO ENSURE THE SUCCESS of your email marketing efforts, it's important to regularly analyze and optimize your email campaigns. Here are some key metrics to track and areas to focus on:

1. **Open Rate**: Monitor the percentage of subscribers who open your emails. A low open rate may indicate issues with your subject lines or sender reputation.

2. **Click-through rate (CTR)**: Measure the percentage of subscribers who click on links within your emails. A low CTR may indicate that your content or CTAs need improvement.

3. **Conversion Rate**: Track the percentage of subscribers who take the desired action, such as making a purchase or signing up for a webinar. Analyze the conversion rate to identify areas for improvement in your email content and CTAs.

4. **Bounce Rate**: Keep an eye on the bounce rate, which

indicates the percentage of emails that were not delivered successfully. High bounce rates may indicate issues with your email list quality or sender reputation.

5. **Unsubscribe Rate**: Monitor the number of subscribers who unsubscribe from your emails. Analyze the reasons behind the unsubscribes and make necessary adjustments to your email content or frequency.

6. **Testing and Optimization**: Continuously test different elements of your emails, such as subject lines, copy, visuals, and CTAs. Use the insights gained from testing to optimize your email campaigns for better results.

By regularly analyzing and optimizing your email campaigns, you can improve engagement, increase conversions, and build stronger relationships with your subscribers.

Implementing effective email marketing is a valuable strategy for home-based businesses to connect with their audience, drive sales, and build a loyal customer base. By building a quality email list, crafting compelling content, leveraging automation and segmentation, and analyzing campaign performance, you can unlock the full potential of email marketing and achieve success in the digital jungle.

Building an Online Presence

5.1 Designing a Professional Website

In today's digital age, having a professional website is essential for any home-based business. Your website serves as the online face of your business, representing your brand and showcasing your products or services to potential customers. It is a powerful tool that can help you establish credibility, attract new clients, and ultimately drive business growth. In this section, we will explore the key elements of designing a professional website that will set you apart from the competition.

5.1.1 Understanding the Importance of Website Design

THE DESIGN OF YOUR website plays a crucial role in creating a positive user experience and leaving a lasting impression on your visitors. A well-designed website not only looks visually appealing but also enhances usability and functionality. It should be easy to navigate, visually engaging, and optimized for different devices and screen sizes.

When designing your website, consider the following elements:

1. Visual Appeal:

CHOOSE A CLEAN AND professional design that aligns with your brand identity. Use high-quality images and graphics that are relevant to your business. Pay attention to color schemes, typography, and overall aesthetics to create a visually pleasing experience for your visitors.

2. User-Friendly Navigation:

ENSURE THAT YOUR WEBSITE is easy to navigate, with clear and intuitive menus. Organize your content into logical sections and provide a search function to help users find what they are looking for quickly. Make sure that important information, such as contact details and product or service descriptions, is easily accessible.

3. Responsive Design:

WITH THE INCREASING use of mobile devices, it is crucial to have a website that is responsive and adapts to different screen sizes. A responsive design ensures that your website looks and functions well on smartphones, tablets, and desktop computers, providing a seamless experience for all users.

4. Page Loading Speed:

OPTIMIZE YOUR WEBSITE'S loading speed to prevent visitors from getting frustrated and leaving. Compress images, minify code, and leverage caching techniques to improve performance. A fast-loading website not only improves the user experience but also positively impacts search engine rankings.

5.1.2 Planning Your Website Structure

BEFORE DIVING INTO the actual design process, it is important to plan the structure and layout of your website. This involves determining the pages and sections you need, as well as the hierarchy and organization of your content. A well-structured website makes it easier for visitors to find information and navigate through your site.

Consider the following steps when planning your website's structure:

1. Identify key pages:

START BY IDENTIFYING the key pages that are essential for your business. This typically includes a homepage, an about page, product or service pages, a contact page, and any additional pages specific to your industry or offerings.

2. Define the navigation menu:

BASED ON THE KEY PAGES you identified, create a clear and concise navigation menu that will be displayed on every page of your website. Use descriptive labels that accurately represent the content of each page.

3. Organize content:

DETERMINE HOW YOU WILL organize your content on each page. Use headings, subheadings, and bullet points to break up the text and make it easier to read. Consider using images, videos, and infographics to enhance the visual appeal and engagement of your content.

4. Create a sitemap:

A SITEMAP IS A VISUAL representation of the structure of your website. It outlines all the pages and their relationships, helping you visualize the flow of information. Creating a sitemap can also assist in identifying any gaps or missing pages in your website structure.

5.1.3 Choosing the Right Content Management System (CMS)

A CONTENT MANAGEMENT system (CMS) is a software platform that allows you to create, manage, and update your website without the need for extensive coding knowledge. Choosing the right CMS is crucial for the long-term success and scalability of your website.

Consider the following popular CMS options:

1. WordPress:

WORDPRESS IS ONE OF the most widely used CMS platforms, known for its flexibility and user-friendly interface. It offers a vast library of themes and plugins, allowing you to customize your website to suit your specific needs. WordPress also has a large community of developers and users, making it easy to find support and resources.

2. Wix:

WIX IS A POPULAR WEBSITE builder that offers a drag-and-drop interface, making it easy for beginners to create a professional website. It provides a range of templates and customization options, allowing you to create a unique and visually appealing website. Wix also offers built-in SEO features and e-commerce capabilities.

3. Shopify:

IF YOU ARE RUNNING an e-commerce business, Shopify is a powerful CMS specifically designed for online stores. It offers a wide range of themes, payment gateways, and inventory management tools. Shopify also provides excellent customer support and integrates seamlessly with various third-party apps and services.

5.1.4 Implementing Effective Website Optimization Techniques

ONCE YOU HAVE DESIGNED your website, it is important to optimize it for search engines to improve its visibility and attract organic traffic. Search engine optimization (SEO) involves various techniques and strategies to enhance your website's ranking in search engine results.

Consider the following SEO techniques:

1. Keyword Research:

IDENTIFY RELEVANT KEYWORDS and phrases that your target audience is likely to search for. Incorporate these keywords naturally into your website's content, including headings, titles, and meta descriptions.

2. On-Page Optimization:

OPTIMIZE EACH PAGE of your website by including relevant keywords in the page title, URL, headings, and content. Ensure that your website's code is clean and follows best practices for SEO.

3. Quality Content:

CREATE HIGH-QUALITY, informative, and engaging content that provides value to your visitors. Regularly update your website with fresh content to keep it relevant and encourage return visits.

4. Link Building:

BUILD HIGH-QUALITY backlinks to your website from reputable sources. This can be achieved through guest blogging, social media promotion, and reaching out to industry influencers for collaborations.

5. Mobile Optimization:

ENSURE THAT YOUR WEBSITE is fully optimized for mobile devices. This includes using responsive design, optimizing images, and improving page loading speed on mobile devices.

By implementing these website optimization techniques, you can improve your website's visibility in search engine results and attract a steady stream of organic traffic.

In conclusion, designing a professional website is a critical step in establishing a strong online presence for your home-based business. By understanding the importance of website design, planning your website structure, choosing the right CMS, and implementing effective optimization techniques, you can create a website that not only looks visually appealing but also drives business growth and success. Remember to regularly update and maintain your website to ensure it remains relevant and engaging to your target audience.

5.2 Optimizing Your Website for Search Engines

IN TODAY'S DIGITAL age, having a strong online presence is crucial for the success of any home-based business. One of the key elements of building an effective online presence is optimizing your website for search engines. Search engine optimization (SEO) is the process of improving your website's visibility and ranking in search engine results pages (SERPs). By implementing SEO strategies, you can increase organic traffic to your website, attract potential customers, and ultimately grow your business.

5.2.1 Understanding Search Engine Optimization

BEFORE DIVING INTO the specifics of optimizing your website, it's important to understand the basics of search engine optimization. Search engines like Google, Bing, and Yahoo use complex algorithms to determine the relevance and quality of websites in relation to specific search queries. These algorithms take into account various factors, such as keywords, website structure, user experience, and backlinks.

The goal of SEO is to align your website with these algorithms, making it easier for search engines to understand and rank your content. By optimizing your website, you can improve its visibility in search engine results, increase organic traffic, and attract potential customers who are actively searching for products or services related to your business.

5.2.2 Conducting Keyword Research

KEYWORDS ARE THE FOUNDATION of SEO. They are the words and phrases that users enter into search engines when looking for information. By conducting thorough keyword research, you can identify the most relevant and valuable keywords for your business. These keywords will then be strategically incorporated into your website's content, meta tags, and URLs.

To conduct keyword research, start by brainstorming a list of words and phrases that are relevant to your business. Think about the products or services you offer, as well as the problems or needs that your target audience may have. Once you have a list of potential keywords, use keyword research tools such as Google Keyword Planner, SEMrush, or Moz Keyword Explorer to analyze their search volume, competition, and relevance.

When selecting keywords, aim for a balance between high search volume and low competition. Long-tail keywords, which are longer and more specific phrases, can often be a valuable strategy for home-based businesses. These keywords may have a lower search volume, but they can attract highly targeted traffic and have a higher chance of conversion.

5.2.3 On-Page Optimization

ON-PAGE OPTIMIZATION refers to the optimization of individual web pages to improve their visibility and ranking in search engine results. It involves optimizing various elements of your website, including content, meta tags, URLs, and internal linking structure.

5.2.3.1 Content Optimization

CONTENT IS KING WHEN it comes to SEO. High-quality, relevant, and engaging content not only attracts visitors but also signals to search engines that your website is valuable and authoritative. When optimizing your content, keep the following tips in mind:

• Incorporate relevant keywords naturally. Sprinkle your chosen keywords throughout your content, including in headings, subheadings, and body text. However, avoid keyword stuffing, as it can negatively impact your website's ranking.

• Write compelling meta descriptions. Meta descriptions are the brief summaries that appear in search engine results. Craft compelling and concise meta descriptions that entice users to click on your website.

• Use descriptive and keyword-rich URLs. Ensure that your URLs are descriptive and contain relevant keywords. For example, instead of using a generic URL like "," use a URL like "."

• Optimize images: Use descriptive file names and alt tags for your images. This helps search engines understand the content of your images and can improve your website's visibility in image search results.

5.2.3.2 Technical Optimization

IN ADDITION TO CONTENT optimization, technical optimization plays a crucial role in improving your website's visibility to search engines. Here are some key technical aspects to consider:

- Mobile optimization: With the increasing use of mobile devices, it's essential to ensure that your website is mobile-friendly. Responsive design, fast loading times, and easy navigation on mobile devices are all important factors for search engine rankings.

- Page speed: Slow-loading websites can negatively impact the user experience and search engine rankings. Optimize your website's loading speed by compressing images, minifying CSS and JavaScript files, and using caching techniques.

- URL structure: Ensure that your website's URLs are clean, concise, and easy to understand. Use hyphens to separate words, and avoid using unnecessary parameters or numbers in your URLs.

- XML sitemap: Create an XML sitemap for your website and submit it to search engines. This helps search engines crawl and index your website more efficiently.

5.2.4 Off-Page Optimization

OFF-PAGE OPTIMIZATION refers to the actions taken outside of your website to improve its visibility and ranking in search engine results. The most important aspect of off-page optimization is building high-quality backlinks to your website. Backlinks are links from other websites that point to your website and are considered a vote of confidence by search engines.

To build backlinks, consider the following strategies:

- Guest blogging: Write high-quality articles for other websites in your industry and include a link back to your website in the author bio or within the content itself.

- Social media promotion: Share your website's content on social media platforms to increase its visibility and encourage others to link back to it.

- Influencer outreach: Collaborate with influencers or industry experts who can promote your website and link back to it from their own platforms.

- Online directories and listings: Submit your website to relevant online directories and listings to increase its visibility and gain backlinks.

Remember, when building backlinks, focus on quality rather than quantity. A few high-quality backlinks from authoritative websites can have a more significant impact on your website's ranking than numerous low-quality backlinks.

5.2.5 Monitoring and Analytics

ONCE YOU HAVE IMPLEMENTED SEO strategies and optimized your website, it's important to monitor your website's performance and analyze the results. This allows you to identify areas for improvement and make data-driven decisions to further optimize your website.

Use web analytics tools such as Google Analytics to track important metrics such as organic traffic, bounce rate, conversion rate, and keyword rankings. Analyze this data regularly to gain insights into user behavior, identify popular content, and make adjustments to your SEO strategy as needed.

By continuously monitoring and analyzing your website's performance, you can stay ahead of the competition, adapt to changing search engine algorithms, and ensure that your website remains optimized for search engines.

Conclusion

OPTIMIZING YOUR WEBSITE for search engines is a critical step in building a strong online presence for your home-based business. By understanding the basics of SEO, conducting keyword research, implementing on-page and off-page optimization strategies, and monitoring your website's performance, you can improve its visibility, attract organic traffic, and ultimately achieve success in the digital jungle. Remember, SEO is an ongoing process, and staying up-to-date with the latest trends and best practices is essential for long-term success.

5.3 Creating Engaging Content

IN TODAY'S DIGITAL landscape, creating engaging content is essential for the success of any home-based business. Engaging content not only attracts and retains the attention of your target audience but also helps to build trust, establish your brand identity, and drive conversions. Whether it's blog posts, social media updates, videos, or podcasts, the content you create should be informative, entertaining, and valuable to your audience. In this section, we will explore the key strategies and techniques for creating engaging content that will captivate your audience and drive your business forward.

5.3.1 Understanding Your Target Audience

BEFORE YOU START CREATING content, it's crucial to have a deep understanding of your target audience. Who are they? What are their needs, interests, and pain points? By understanding your audience, you can tailor your content to meet their specific needs and preferences. Conduct market research, analyze customer data, and engage with your audience through surveys or social media to gather insights about their preferences and interests. This information will help you create content that resonates with your target audience and keeps them engaged.

5.3.2 Defining Your Content Strategy

A WELL-DEFINED CONTENT strategy is the foundation for creating engaging content. It outlines your goals, target audience, key messages, and the platforms you will use to distribute your content. Start by setting clear objectives for your content, whether it's to educate, entertain, inspire, or promote your products or services. Then, identify the topics and themes that align with your brand and resonate with your audience. Develop a content calendar to plan and organize your content creation efforts, ensuring a consistent flow of engaging content.

5.3.3 Crafting Compelling Headlines

THE HEADLINE IS THE first thing your audience sees, and it plays a crucial role in capturing their attention. A compelling headline should be concise, intriguing, and promise value to the reader. Use power words, numbers, and emotional triggers to make your headlines more compelling. Experiment with different headline formulas and test their performance to see what resonates best with your audience. Remember, a great headline can make the difference between your content being ignored or clicked on.

5.3.4 Telling Stories

HUMANS ARE WIRED TO connect with stories. Incorporating storytelling into your content can make it more relatable, memorable, and engaging. Share personal anecdotes, case studies, or customer success stories that demonstrate the value of your products or services. Use storytelling techniques such as creating a narrative arc, using vivid descriptions, and evoking emotions to captivate your audience. By weaving stories into your content, you can create a deeper connection with your audience and leave a lasting impression.

5.3.5 Providing Valuable Information

ONE OF THE KEY ELEMENTS of engaging content is providing valuable information to your audience. Your content should aim to educate, inform, or solve a problem for your readers. Conduct thorough research, gather data, and provide insights that are not readily available elsewhere. Share your expertise and offer practical tips, advice, or tutorials that your audience can apply to their lives or businesses. By consistently delivering valuable information, you position yourself as a trusted authority in your industry and keep your audience coming back for more.

5.3.6 Using Visuals and Multimedia

VISUAL CONTENT IS HIGHLY engaging and can help to break up text-heavy content. Incorporate relevant images, infographics, videos, and other multimedia elements into your content to make it more visually appealing and interactive. Visuals can help convey complex information in a more digestible format and capture the attention of your audience. Ensure that your visuals are high-quality, on-brand, and enhance the overall message of your content.

5.3.7 Encouraging Interaction and Engagement

ENGAGING CONTENT SHOULD encourage interaction and engagement from your audience. Include calls-to-action (CTAs) in your content to prompt your readers to take a specific action, such as leaving a comment, sharing the content, or subscribing to your newsletter. Respond to comments and engage with your audience to foster a sense of community and build relationships. Encourage user-generated content by running contests, asking for feedback, or featuring customer testimonials. By actively involving your audience, you create a more interactive and engaging experience.

5.3.8 Optimizing for Search Engines

CREATING ENGAGING CONTENT is not just about captivating your audience; it's also about ensuring that your content is discoverable by search engines. Incorporate relevant keywords and meta tags, and optimize your content for search engine optimization (SEO) to improve its visibility in search engine results. Conduct keyword research to identify the terms and phrases your audience is searching for and strategically incorporate them into your content. By optimizing your content for search engines, you increase the chances of attracting organic traffic and reaching a wider audience.

5.3.9 Analyzing and Iterating

CREATING ENGAGING CONTENT is an ongoing process of learning and improvement. Regularly analyze the performance of your content using analytics tools to understand what is resonating with your audience and what is not. Track metrics such as page views, time on page, social shares, and conversion rates to gauge the effectiveness of your content. Use this data to iterate and refine your content strategy, focusing on creating more of what works and adjusting or eliminating what doesn't. By continuously analyzing and iterating, you can create content that consistently engages and delights your audience.

Creating engaging content is a continuous journey that requires creativity, research, and a deep understanding of your audience. By following the strategies and techniques outlined in this section, you can create content that captivates your audience, builds your brand, and drives the success of your home-based business in the digital jungle.

5.4 Harnessing the Power of Blogging

IN TODAY'S DIGITAL age, blogging has become an essential tool for individuals and businesses alike. It provides a platform for sharing knowledge, expressing ideas, and connecting with a global audience. For home-based entrepreneurs, blogging can be a powerful tool to establish credibility, build a loyal following, and ultimately drive business growth. In this section, we will explore the benefits of blogging and provide practical tips on how to harness its power for home-based success.

5.4.1 Establishing Your Blogging Strategy

BEFORE DIVING INTO the world of blogging, it's important to establish a clear strategy. This involves defining your target audience, identifying your blogging goals, and determining the frequency and topics of your blog posts.

Defining Your Target Audience

UNDERSTANDING YOUR target audience is crucial for creating content that resonates with them. Take the time to research and identify the demographics, interests, and pain points of your ideal readers. This will help you tailor your blog posts to their needs and preferences, increasing the chances of engagement and conversion.

Identifying Your Blogging Goals

WHAT DO YOU HOPE TO achieve through your blog? Are you looking to establish yourself as an industry expert, drive traffic to your website, or generate leads? Clearly defining your blogging goals will guide your content creation and help you measure the success of your efforts.

Determining the Frequency and Topics of Your Blog Posts

CONSISTENCY IS KEY when it comes to blogging. Determine how often you can realistically publish new content and stick to a regular schedule. This will help you build a loyal readership and improve your search engine rankings. Additionally, brainstorm a list of topics that align with your target audience's interests and your expertise. This will ensure that you always have a pool of ideas to draw from when creating new blog posts.

5.4.2 Creating Engaging and Valuable Content

THE SUCCESS OF YOUR blog ultimately depends on the quality of your content. To attract and retain readers, it's important to create engaging and valuable blog posts that provide solutions, insights, or entertainment. Here are some tips to help you create compelling content:

Understand your readers' needs.

PUT YOURSELF IN YOUR readers' shoes and think about what they would find valuable. What are their pain points, challenges, or questions? By addressing these needs in your blog posts, you will establish yourself as a trusted resource and keep your readers coming back for more.

Provide actionable tips and advice.

ONE OF THE BEST WAYS to add value to your blog posts is by providing actionable tips and advice. Share your expertise and insights, and offer practical steps that your readers can implement in their own lives or businesses. This will not only position you as an authority in your field but also encourage engagement and social sharing.

Use a conversational tone.

BLOGGING IS A MORE informal medium compared to traditional writing. Use a conversational tone in your blog posts to connect with your readers on a personal level. Write as if you're having a conversation with a friend, and avoid using jargon or overly technical language that may alienate your audience.

Incorporate visuals and multimedia.

TO MAKE YOUR BLOG POSTS more engaging, consider incorporating visuals and multimedia elements such as images, videos, infographics, or slideshows. Visual content not only breaks up the text but also helps to convey information more effectively and capture your readers' attention.

5.4.3 Promoting Your Blog

CREATING GREAT CONTENT is only half the battle. To maximize the reach and impact of your blog, you need to promote it effectively. Here are some strategies to help you get your blog in front of a wider audience:

Utilize social media platforms.

SOCIAL MEDIA PLATFORMS such as Facebook, Twitter, LinkedIn, and Instagram are powerful tools for promoting your blog. Share your blog posts on these platforms, engage with your followers, and encourage them to share your content with their networks. Additionally, join relevant groups and communities where your target audience hangs out and actively participate in discussions.

Guest Blogging

GUEST BLOGGING INVOLVES writing and publishing articles on other websites or blogs within your industry. This allows you to tap into an existing audience and gain exposure to new readers. Look for reputable blogs that accept guest posts and pitch them with your ideas. Make sure to provide high-quality content that aligns with their audience's interests.

Search Engine Optimization (SEO)

OPTIMIZING YOUR BLOG posts for search engines can significantly increase your visibility and organic traffic. Conduct keyword research to identify relevant keywords and incorporate them naturally into your blog posts. Additionally, optimize your meta tags, headings, and URLs to improve your search engine rankings.

Engage with your readers.

BUILDING A LOYAL READERSHIP requires engaging with your audience. Respond to comments on your blog posts, encourage discussion, and ask for feedback. This not only shows that you value your readers' opinions but also helps to foster a sense of community around your blog.

5.4.4 Monetizing Your Blog

WHILE BLOGGING CAN be a fulfilling creative outlet, it can also be a source of income. Here are some ways to monetize your blog:

Affiliate Marketing

AFFILIATE MARKETING involves promoting products or services on your blog and earning a commission for each sale or lead generated through your referral. Join affiliate programs that align with your blog's niche and recommend products or services that you genuinely believe in.

Sponsored Content

AS YOUR BLOG GROWS in popularity, you may have the opportunity to collaborate with brands and businesses for sponsored content. This involves creating blog posts or reviews that promote their products or services in exchange for compensation. Make sure to disclose any sponsored content to maintain transparency with your readers.

Digital Products

IF YOU HAVE SPECIALIZED knowledge or expertise, consider creating and selling digital products such as e-books, online courses, or templates. This allows you to monetize your expertise and provide additional value to your readers.

Advertising

ONCE YOUR BLOG HAS a significant amount of traffic, you can monetize it through display advertising. Join ad networks such as Google AdSense or Mediavine and display ads on your blog. However, be mindful of the balance between ads and the user experience, as excessive advertising can deter readers.

In conclusion, blogging is a powerful tool for home-based entrepreneurs to establish credibility, build a loyal following, and drive business growth. By creating engaging and valuable content, promoting your blog effectively, and exploring monetization opportunities, you can harness the power of blogging to achieve home-based success in the digital jungle.

Managing Finances and Taxes

6.1 Tracking Income and Expenses

One of the most important aspects of running a successful home-based business is effectively tracking your income and expenses. By keeping accurate records of your financial transactions, you can gain valuable insights into the financial health of your business, make informed decisions, and ensure compliance with tax obligations. In this section, we will explore the importance of tracking income and expenses and provide practical tips on how to do it efficiently.

6.1.1 Why Tracking Income and Expenses is Crucial

TRACKING YOUR INCOME and expenses is crucial for several reasons. Firstly, it allows you to have a clear understanding of your business's financial performance. By regularly reviewing your income and expenses, you can identify trends, spot areas for improvement, and make informed decisions to optimize your profitability.

Secondly, accurate tracking of income and expenses is essential for tax purposes. As a home-based business owner, you are required to report your income and expenses to the tax authorities. By maintaining detailed records, you can ensure that you are accurately reporting your income and claiming all eligible deductions, thereby minimizing your tax liability and avoiding potential penalties.

Furthermore, tracking your income and expenses provides you with a comprehensive financial overview of your business. It enables you to analyze your cash flow, identify areas of overspending or underspending, and make adjustments to your budget accordingly. This level of financial visibility is crucial for maintaining the financial stability and sustainability of your home-based business.

6.1.2 Establishing a System for Tracking Income and Expenses

TO EFFECTIVELY TRACK your income and expenses, it is essential to establish a systematic approach. Here are some steps to help you set up a reliable system:

6.1.2.1 Separate Business and Personal Finances

ONE OF THE FIRST STEPS in tracking your income and expenses is to separate your business and personal finances. Open a separate bank account and credit card specifically for your business transactions. This separation will make it easier to track and categorize your business expenses, ensuring accuracy and simplifying the tax reporting process.

6.1.2.2 Choose an Accounting Method

THERE ARE TWO PRIMARY accounting methods: cash basis and accrual basis. The cash basis method records income and expenses when cash is received or paid, while the accrual basis method records income and expenses when they are earned or incurred, regardless of cash flow. Choose the method that best suits your business needs and consult with a financial professional if necessary.

6.1.2.3 Utilize Accounting Software

INVESTING IN ACCOUNTING software can greatly simplify the process of tracking income and expenses. There are numerous software options available, ranging from basic to advanced features. Look for software that allows you to categorize transactions, generate financial reports, and integrate with other business tools. Popular accounting software options include QuickBooks, Xero, and FreshBooks.

6.1.2.4 Create a chart of accounts.

A CHART OF ACCOUNTS is a categorized list of all the accounts used in your business's financial transactions. It provides a structured framework for organizing and tracking income and expenses. Create a chart of accounts that aligns with your business's specific needs and industry requirements. Common account categories include revenue, cost of goods sold, operating expenses, and assets.

6.1.2.5 Regularly Record Transactions

CONSISTENCY IS KEY when it comes to tracking income and expenses. Make it a habit to record all financial transactions promptly and accurately. This includes income from sales, payments received, expenses incurred, and bills paid. Set aside dedicated time each week or month to update your accounting records, ensuring that no transactions are missed or overlooked.

6.1.3 Categorizing Income and Expenses

CATEGORIZING YOUR INCOME and expenses is essential for accurate financial tracking and reporting. By assigning each transaction to the appropriate category, you can gain a clear understanding of where your money is coming from and where it is going. Here are some common categories to consider:

6.1.3.1 Income Categories

- Sales revenue
- Service fees
- Rental income
- Affiliate commissions
- Royalties

6.1.3.2 Expense Categories

- Office supplies

- Advertising and marketing
- Utilities
- Rent or mortgage
- Professional fees
- Travel and transportation
- Insurance
- Taxes

CUSTOMIZE THESE CATEGORIES based on your specific business needs and industry requirements. Regularly review and update your categories as your business evolves and new expenses arise.

6.1.4 Maintaining Documentation

IN ADDITION TO TRACKING income and expenses in your accounting software, it is crucial to maintain supporting documentation. This documentation serves as evidence of your financial transactions and can be invaluable during tax audits or financial reviews. Here are some important documents to keep:

- Invoices and receipts
- Bank and credit card statements
- Contracts and agreements
- Payroll records
- Tax forms and filings

Organize these documents in a systematic manner, either physically or digitally, to ensure easy access and retrieval when needed.

6.1.5 Reviewing and Analyzing Financial Reports

REGULARLY REVIEWING and analyzing financial reports is essential for gaining insights into your business's financial performance. Most accounting software provides standard financial reports such as profit and loss statements, balance sheets, and cash flow statements. These reports can help you identify trends, assess profitability, and make informed decisions to drive the growth of your home-based business.

When reviewing financial reports, pay attention to key performance indicators (KPIs) such as gross profit margin, net profit margin, and return on investment (ROI). These metrics can provide valuable insights into the financial health and efficiency of your business.

6.1.6 Seeking Professional Financial Advice

WHILE TRACKING INCOME and expenses is something you can do on your own, seeking professional financial advice can provide additional guidance and expertise. Consider consulting with a certified public accountant (CPA) or a financial advisor who specializes in small businesses. They can help you navigate complex tax regulations, optimize your financial processes, and provide strategic advice to help you achieve long-term financial success.

By effectively tracking your income and expenses, you can gain a clear understanding of your business's financial health, make informed decisions, and ensure compliance with tax obligations. Implementing a systematic approach, utilizing accounting software, and seeking professional advice when needed will set you on the path to financial success in your home-based business.

6.2 Understanding Tax Obligations

WHEN IT COMES TO RUNNING a home-based business, understanding your tax obligations is crucial. Taxes can be complex and overwhelming, but with the right knowledge and preparation, you can navigate the tax landscape with confidence. In this section, we will explore the various tax obligations that home-based entrepreneurs need to be aware of and provide you with practical tips to ensure compliance and maximize your tax benefits.

6.2.1 Types of Taxes

AS A HOME-BASED BUSINESS owner, you will encounter different types of taxes that you need to understand and fulfill. Here are some of the most common tax obligations:

Income Tax

INCOME TAX IS THE TAX you pay on the profits generated by your business. It is important to keep accurate records of your income and expenses to determine your taxable income. Depending on your jurisdiction, you may be required to file income tax returns annually or quarterly.

Self-Employment Tax

IF YOU ARE SELF-EMPLOYED, you are responsible for paying self-employment tax, which covers your contributions to Social Security and Medicare. Unlike traditional employees, who have these taxes withheld from their paychecks, self-employed individuals must calculate and pay these taxes themselves.

Sales Tax

IF YOUR HOME-BASED business involves selling products or services, you may be required to collect and remit sales tax. The rules and regulations regarding sales tax vary by jurisdiction, so it is essential to research and understand the requirements specific to your location.

Employment Taxes

IF YOU HAVE EMPLOYEES working for your home-based business, you will have additional tax obligations related to employment. These include withholding and remitting payroll taxes, such as federal and state income tax, Social Security tax, and Medicare tax.

6.2.2 Registering for Taxes

TO ENSURE COMPLIANCE with tax laws, it is important to register for the necessary tax accounts. Here are the steps you should take:

Obtain an employer identification number (EIN).

AN EIN IS A UNIQUE identifier for your business, similar to a Social Security number. You will need an EIN if you have employees or if your business is structured as a partnership or corporation. You can apply for an EIN online through the Internal Revenue Service's (IRS) website.

Register for state and local taxes.

DEPENDING ON YOUR LOCATION, you may need to register for state and local taxes, such as sales tax or business income tax. Check with your state and local tax authorities to determine the specific requirements and registration process.

6.2.3 Recordkeeping and Documentation

MAINTAINING ACCURATE and organized financial records is essential for fulfilling your tax obligations. Here are some best practices for recordkeeping:

Separate business and personal finances

TO SIMPLIFY YOUR RECORDKEEPING and ensure accurate reporting, it is crucial to keep your business and personal finances separate. Open a separate bank account for your business and use it exclusively for business transactions.

Keep detailed records of income and expenses.

KEEP TRACK OF ALL YOUR business income and expenses. This includes sales receipts, invoices, bank statements, and any other relevant financial documents. Use accounting software or spreadsheets to record and categorize your transactions.

Retain records for the appropriate time period.

DIFFERENT TYPES OF records should be retained for specific periods. For example, tax returns and supporting documents should generally be kept for at least three years. However, it is advisable to consult with a tax professional or refer to the guidelines provided by your tax authority to determine the specific record retention requirements.

6.2.4 Tax Deductions and Credits

ONE OF THE BENEFITS of running a home-based business is the opportunity to take advantage of various tax deductions and credits. Here are some common deductions and credits that may apply to your business:

Home Office Deduction

IF YOU USE A PORTION of your home exclusively for your business, you may be eligible for a home office deduction. This deduction allows you to deduct a portion of your home-related expenses, such as rent, mortgage interest, utilities, and insurance.

Business Expenses

YOU CAN DEDUCT ORDINARY and necessary business expenses, such as office supplies, equipment, marketing expenses, professional fees, and travel expenses. Keep detailed records and receipts to support your deductions.

Health Insurance Deduction

IF YOU ARE SELF-EMPLOYED and pay for your own health insurance, you may be eligible to deduct the premiums as a business expense. Consult with a tax professional to determine if you qualify for this deduction.

Retirement Contributions

AS A SELF-EMPLOYED individual, you have the opportunity to contribute to retirement plans specifically designed for small business owners, such as a Simplified Employee Pension (SEP) IRA or a Solo 401(k). Contributions to these plans are tax-deductible and can help you save for retirement while reducing your taxable income.

6.2.5 Seeking Professional Tax Advice

NAVIGATING THE COMPLEXITIES of taxes can be challenging, especially if you are unfamiliar with the tax laws and regulations. Consider seeking professional tax advice from a certified public accountant (CPA) or a tax attorney who specializes in small business taxation. A tax professional can help you understand your specific tax obligations, identify potential deductions and credits, and ensure compliance with tax laws.

Remember, staying informed and proactive about your tax obligations is essential for the long-term success of your home-based business. By understanding the types of taxes you need to pay, registering for the necessary tax accounts, maintaining accurate records, and seeking professional advice when needed, you can navigate the tax landscape with confidence and maximize your tax benefits.

6.3 Organizing Financial Records

ONE OF THE KEY ASPECTS of running a successful home-based business is effectively managing your finances. As a home-based entrepreneur, it is crucial to keep track of your income, expenses, and financial records to ensure the smooth operation of your business. Organizing your financial records not only helps you stay on top of your finances but also enables you to make informed decisions and meet your tax obligations. In this section, we will explore some essential strategies for organizing your financial records and maintaining financial harmony in your digital jungle.

6.3.1 Separate Business and Personal Finances

TO MAINTAIN CLARITY and accuracy in your financial records, it is essential to separate your business and personal finances. Mixing personal and business expenses can lead to confusion and make it challenging to track your business's financial health. By opening a separate bank account for your business and using it exclusively for business-related transactions, you can easily differentiate between personal and business expenses. This separation will simplify your record-keeping process and provide a clear picture of your business's financial performance.

6.3.2 Choose an Accounting System

SELECTING THE RIGHT accounting system is crucial for organizing your financial records effectively. There are various accounting software options available that cater to the needs of home-based businesses. These software solutions offer features such as expense tracking, invoicing, financial reporting, and tax preparation. Consider your business's specific requirements and choose an accounting system that aligns with your needs and budget. Implementing an accounting system will streamline your financial management process and provide you with accurate and up-to-date financial information.

6.3.3 Maintain a Chart of Accounts

A CHART OF ACCOUNTS is a categorized list of all the accounts used in your business's financial transactions. It provides a systematic way to organize and track your income, expenses, assets, and liabilities. Creating a chart of accounts tailored to your business will help you categorize your financial transactions accurately. Common account categories include revenue, cost of goods sold, operating expenses, assets, and liabilities. By maintaining a well-structured chart of accounts, you can easily generate financial reports and analyze your business's financial performance.

6.3.4 Implement a Record-Keeping System

ESTABLISHING A RECORD-keeping system is essential for maintaining organized financial records. This system should include a method for storing and organizing your financial documents, such as receipts, invoices, bank statements, and tax records. Consider using digital tools like cloud storage or accounting software to store and organize your financial documents securely. Create a logical folder structure and consistently name your files to ensure easy retrieval when needed. Regularly update your record-keeping system to keep it organized and up-to-date.

6.3.5 Track Income and Expenses

ACCURATELY TRACKING your income and expenses is vital for understanding your business's financial health. Keep a record of all your business-related income sources, including sales, services rendered, and any other sources of revenue. Similarly, diligently track your business expenses, including purchases, subscriptions, utilities, and any other costs incurred in running your business. By maintaining a detailed record of your income and expenses, you can monitor your cash flow, identify areas for improvement, and make informed financial decisions.

6.3.6 Regularly Reconcile Bank Statements

RECONCILING YOUR BANK statements is an essential practice to ensure the accuracy of your financial records. Regularly compare your bank statements with your accounting records to identify any discrepancies or errors. This process involves matching the transactions recorded in your accounting system with the transactions listed in your bank statement. By reconciling your bank statements, you can identify any missing or duplicate transactions, detect potential fraud, and maintain the integrity of your financial records.

6.3.7 Keep Track of Tax Obligations

AS A HOME-BASED BUSINESS owner, it is crucial to stay on top of your tax obligations. Keep track of important tax deadlines and ensure the timely filing of your tax returns. Maintain accurate records of your income, expenses, and any relevant tax documents, such as receipts and invoices. By organizing your financial records and staying informed about tax regulations, you can minimize the risk of errors, penalties, and audits. Consider consulting with a tax professional to ensure compliance with tax laws and maximize your tax deductions.

6.3.8 Regularly Review and Analyze Financial Reports

FINANCIAL REPORTS PROVIDE valuable insights into your business's financial performance and help you make informed decisions. Regularly review and analyze financial reports such as profit and loss statements, balance sheets, and cash flow statements. These reports will give you a comprehensive overview of your business's revenue, expenses, assets, and liabilities. By analyzing these reports, you can identify trends, assess the profitability of your business, and make the necessary adjustments to achieve your financial goals.

6.3.9 Back Up Your Financial Records

PROTECTING YOUR FINANCIAL records is crucial to ensuring the continuity of your business operations. Regularly back up your financial records to prevent data loss in case of hardware failure, theft, or other unforeseen events. Consider using cloud storage or external hard drives to create backups of your financial documents and accounting software. Implementing a robust backup system will provide you with peace of mind and ensure that your financial records are secure and accessible when needed.

6.3.10 Seek Professional Financial Advice

MANAGING YOUR FINANCES effectively can be challenging, especially if you are not familiar with accounting principles and tax regulations. Consider seeking professional financial advice from an accountant or bookkeeper who specializes in working with home-based businesses. A financial professional can provide guidance on organizing your financial records, optimizing your tax deductions, and ensuring compliance with financial regulations. Their expertise will help you navigate the complexities of financial management and enable you to focus on growing your home-based business.

By implementing these strategies for organizing your financial records, you can establish a solid foundation for financial success in your home-based business. Maintaining accurate and organized financial records will not only help you make informed decisions but also ensure compliance with tax regulations and provide a clear picture of your business's financial health. Embrace the digital tools and systems available to streamline your financial management process and achieve harmony in the financial aspect of your digital jungle.

6.4 Seeking Professional Financial Advice

WHEN IT COMES TO MANAGING finances and taxes for your home-based business, seeking professional financial advice can be a game-changer. While you may have a good understanding of your business and its financial aspects, consulting with a financial expert can provide you with valuable insights and guidance to ensure your financial success.

6.4.1 The Importance of Professional Financial Advice

RUNNING A HOME-BASED business requires careful financial planning and management. From tracking income and expenses to understanding tax obligations, there are various financial aspects that need to be handled efficiently.

Seeking professional financial advice can help you navigate through these complexities and make informed decisions that can have a significant impact on the financial health of your business.

Here are some key reasons why seeking professional financial advice is crucial for home-based business owners:

Expertise and knowledge

FINANCIAL ADVISORS are trained professionals who have in-depth knowledge and expertise in various financial matters. They can provide you with valuable insights and advice based on their experience and understanding of the financial landscape. By leveraging their expertise, you can gain a better understanding of your financial situation and make informed decisions that align with your business goals.

Tax planning and optimization

ONE OF THE MOST CRITICAL aspects of managing finances for your home-based business is understanding and optimizing your tax obligations. A financial advisor can help you navigate through the complex tax laws and regulations, ensuring that you are taking advantage of all available deductions and credits. They can also assist you in developing a tax planning strategy that minimizes your tax liability while remaining compliant with the law.

Financial Goal Setting and Planning

SETTING FINANCIAL GOALS and developing a comprehensive financial plan are essential for the long-term success of your home-based business. A financial advisor can help you define your financial goals, create a realistic plan to achieve them, and monitor your progress along the way. They can provide valuable insights and recommendations to ensure that your financial plan aligns with your business objectives and helps you achieve sustainable growth.

Risk Management

RUNNING A BUSINESS involves inherent risks, and it is crucial to have a solid risk management strategy in place. A financial advisor can assess your business's risk profile and help you develop strategies to mitigate potential risks. They can also guide you in selecting appropriate insurance coverage to protect your business from unforeseen events and liabilities.

Retirement Planning

AS A HOME-BASED BUSINESS owner, planning for your retirement is essential. A financial advisor can help you develop a retirement plan that takes into account your business's financials, personal financial goals, and the lifestyle you envision for your retirement years. They can guide you in selecting the right retirement accounts and investment options to ensure a secure and comfortable retirement.

6.4.2 Finding the Right Financial Advisor

FINDING THE RIGHT FINANCIAL advisor for your home-based business is crucial for a successful partnership. Here are some steps to help you find the right professional:

Assess your needs.

BEFORE YOU START SEARCHING for a financial advisor, take the time to assess your specific needs and requirements. Consider the areas where you need the most assistance, such as tax planning, retirement planning, or general financial management. This will help you narrow down your search and find an advisor who specializes in the areas that are most relevant to your business.

Research and referrals

START YOUR SEARCH BY conducting thorough research. Look for financial advisors who have experience working with home-based businesses or entrepreneurs. Read reviews and testimonials from their clients to get an idea of their expertise and the quality of their services. Additionally, ask for referrals from other business owners or professionals in your network who have had positive experiences with financial advisors.

Credentials and experience

WHEN EVALUATING POTENTIAL financial advisors, consider their credentials and experience. Look for professionals who hold relevant certifications, such as Certified Financial Planner (CFP) or Chartered Financial Analyst (CFA). These certifications indicate that the advisor has met specific educational and ethical standards. Additionally, consider the advisor's experience working with businesses similar to yours and their track record of success.

Compatibility and communication

BUILDING A STRONG WORKING relationship with your financial advisor is essential. During the initial consultation, assess the advisor's communication style and determine if it aligns with your preferences. Ensure that they are responsive, attentive, and willing to listen to your concerns and goals. A good financial advisor should be able to explain complex financial concepts in a way that you can understand and feel comfortable with.

Fee Structure

FINANCIAL ADVISORS charge fees for their services, and it is essential to understand their fee structure before entering into an agreement. Some advisors charge a percentage of the assets they manage, while others charge an hourly or flat fee. Discuss the fee structure with potential advisors and ensure that it aligns with your budget and the value you expect to receive from their services.

6.4.3 Maximizing the Benefits of Professional Financial Advice

ONCE YOU HAVE FOUND the right financial advisor for your home-based business, it is essential to maximize the benefits of their expertise. Here are some tips to make the most of your partnership:

Open and honest communication

MAINTAIN OPEN AND HONEST communication with your financial advisor. Share all relevant information about your business, financial goals, and any changes in your circumstances. The more your advisor knows about your situation, the better they can tailor their advice and recommendations to meet your specific needs.

Regular reviews and updates

SCHEDULE REGULAR REVIEWS and updates with your financial advisor to assess the progress of your financial plan and make any necessary adjustments. As your business evolves, your financial goals may change, and it is crucial to keep your advisor informed. Regular reviews will ensure that your financial plan remains aligned with your business objectives.

Act on Recommendations

YOUR FINANCIAL ADVISOR will provide you with recommendations and strategies to improve your financial situation. Act on these recommendations promptly and implement the suggested changes. Remember that the value of professional financial advice lies in taking action based on the expert guidance you receive.

Stay Informed

WHILE YOUR FINANCIAL advisor is there to guide you, it is essential to stay informed about financial matters related to your business. Educate yourself about basic financial concepts, tax laws, and investment strategies. This will enable you to have meaningful discussions with your advisor and make informed decisions about your business's financial future.

Conclusion

SEEKING PROFESSIONAL financial advice is a wise investment for home-based business owners. A financial advisor can provide you with the expertise, guidance, and support you need to navigate the financial complexities of running a business. By finding the right advisor and maximizing the benefits of their services, you can ensure the long-term financial success of your home-based business.

Building a
Supportive Network

7.1 Connecting with Like-Minded Entrepreneurs

As a home-based entrepreneur, it can sometimes feel isolating to work alone. However, one of the keys to success in the digital jungle is building a supportive network of like-minded entrepreneurs. Connecting with others who understand the challenges and triumphs of running a home-based business can provide valuable insights, support, and inspiration. In this section, we will explore various ways to connect with like-minded entrepreneurs and build a strong support system.

7.1.1 Joining Online Communities and Forums

THE INTERNET HAS MADE it easier than ever to connect with people from all over the world who share similar interests and goals. Online communities and forums dedicated to entrepreneurship and home-based businesses are a great place to start. These platforms provide a space for entrepreneurs to ask questions, share experiences, and learn from one another.

When joining an online community or forum, take the time to introduce yourself and share a bit about your business. Engage in conversations, offer advice, and ask for help when needed. By actively participating in these communities, you can establish yourself as a valuable member and build meaningful connections with other entrepreneurs.

7.1.2 Attending Networking Events

WHILE ONLINE COMMUNITIES are convenient, there is still immense value in face-to-face interactions. Attending networking events specifically tailored for entrepreneurs can provide opportunities to meet like-minded individuals, exchange ideas, and form valuable connections.

Research local networking events in your area or consider attending industry-specific conferences and trade shows. These events often feature workshops, panel discussions, and networking sessions designed to facilitate meaningful connections. Be prepared to introduce yourself and your business, and don't be afraid to strike up conversations with fellow attendees. Remember, everyone is there for the same reason: to connect and grow their network.

7.1.3 Finding Mentors and Coaches

HAVING A MENTOR OR coach can be incredibly beneficial for your personal and professional growth. Mentors are experienced entrepreneurs who can provide guidance, advice, and support based on their own experiences. They can help you navigate challenges, make informed decisions, and offer valuable insights into the industry.

To find a mentor, start by identifying successful entrepreneurs in your field or industry. Reach out to them and express your admiration for their work. Explain your goals and aspirations, and ask if they would be willing to mentor you. While not everyone will have the time or capacity to take on a mentee, you may be surprised by how many entrepreneurs are willing to share their knowledge and support others.

If finding a mentor proves challenging, consider hiring a business coach. Coaches specialize in helping entrepreneurs overcome obstacles, set goals, and develop strategies for success. They can provide personalized guidance and hold you accountable for your actions. Look for coaches who have experience working with home-based entrepreneurs and who align with your values and goals.

7.1.4 Collaborating with Peers

COLLABORATION IS A powerful tool for growth and innovation. By partnering with like-minded entrepreneurs, you can combine your skills, knowledge, and resources to achieve mutual success. Collaboration can take many forms, such as joint ventures, co-creating products or services, or even sharing marketing efforts.

To find potential collaborators, reach out to entrepreneurs in complementary industries or those who share a similar target audience. Attend industry events or join online groups where you can connect with potential collaborators. Approach these conversations with a mindset of mutual benefit and be open to exploring different possibilities.

When collaborating, clearly define roles, responsibilities, and expectations from the outset. Establish open lines of communication and maintain transparency throughout the process. By working together, you can leverage each other's strengths and create innovative solutions that benefit both parties.

7.1.5 Building Genuine Relationships

WHILE NETWORKING AND connecting with other entrepreneurs can be beneficial for your business, it's important to approach these relationships with authenticity and a genuine desire to connect. Building meaningful relationships takes time and effort, so focus on quality over quantity.

Take the time to get to know other entrepreneurs on a personal level. Show a genuine interest in their businesses and experiences. Offer support and celebrate their successes. By nurturing these relationships, you can create a strong support system that will be there for you during both the highs and lows of your entrepreneurial journey.

Remember, building a supportive network is not just about what you can gain from others. It's also about what you can contribute. Be willing to share your knowledge, offer assistance, and provide support to fellow entrepreneurs. By fostering a culture of collaboration and support, you can create a thriving community of like-minded individuals who uplift and inspire one another.

In the next section, we will explore the importance of attending networking events and how they can help you expand your network and grow your business.

7.2 Joining Online Communities and

Forums

IN TODAY'S DIGITAL age, connecting with like-minded individuals and building a supportive network is crucial for the success of any home-based business. While working from home offers flexibility and freedom, it can also be isolating at times. That's why joining online communities and forums can be a game-changer for entrepreneurs seeking support, advice, and collaboration.

7.2.1 The Power of Online Communities

ONLINE COMMUNITIES and forums provide a platform for entrepreneurs to connect, share experiences, and learn from one another. These virtual spaces bring together individuals with similar interests, goals, and challenges, creating a sense of belonging and camaraderie. By joining these communities, home-based business owners can tap into a wealth of knowledge, resources, and opportunities.

7.2.2 Finding the Right Online Communities

WITH COUNTLESS ONLINE communities and forums available, it's important to find the ones that align with your business niche and goals. Here are some tips to help you find the right communities to join:

1. Research: Take the time to research and explore different online communities and forums. Look for platforms that cater to your industry or specific business niche. Consider factors such as the size of the community, the level of engagement, and the

quality of discussions.

2. Ask for Recommendations: Reach out to fellow entrepreneurs, colleagues, or mentors and ask for recommendations on online communities they find valuable. They may be able to point you in the direction of communities that have been instrumental in their own success.

3. Read Reviews and Testimonials: Look for reviews and testimonials from other members of the online communities you are considering. This will give you insights into the community's culture, the level of support provided, and the overall experience of its members.

4. Participate in Trial Periods: Many online communities offer trial periods or free memberships. Take advantage of these opportunities to get a feel for the community and determine if it aligns with your needs and expectations.

7.2.3 Benefits of Joining Online Communities and Forums

JOINING ONLINE COMMUNITIES and forums can offer numerous benefits for home-based business owners. Here are some of the advantages:

1. Networking Opportunities: Online communities provide a platform to connect with like-minded entrepreneurs, potential clients, and industry experts. By actively participating in discussions and sharing your expertise, you can expand your network and

build valuable relationships.

2. Support and Advice: Running a home-based business can be challenging, and having a support system is crucial. Online communities offer a space where you can seek advice, share your struggles, and receive support from individuals who understand the unique challenges of working from home.

3. Learning and Growth: Online communities are a treasure trove of knowledge and expertise. By engaging in discussions, asking questions, and sharing your own insights, you can learn from others' experiences and gain valuable insights to help you grow your business.

4. Collaboration Opportunities: Online communities often foster collaboration among members. By connecting with individuals who complement your skills and expertise, you can explore partnership opportunities, joint ventures, and collaborations that can benefit both parties involved.

5. Access to Resources and Opportunities: Many online communities share valuable resources, such as industry reports, templates, and tools. Additionally, members often share job opportunities, client referrals, and other business prospects, creating a supportive ecosystem for growth.

7.2.4 Best Practices for Engaging in Online Communities

TO MAKE THE MOST OF your online community experience, it's important to follow some best practices:

1. Be Active and Engaged: Actively participate in discussions, share your knowledge, and contribute to the community. The more engaged you are, the more you will benefit from the collective wisdom of the community.

2. Give and Receive: Remember that online communities are built on reciprocity. Offer support, advice, and assistance to others whenever possible. In return, you will receive the same level of support and build stronger relationships within the community.

3. Respect the Community Guidelines: Each online community has its own set of guidelines and rules. Familiarize yourself with these guidelines, and ensure that your interactions align with the community's values and expectations.

4. Be authentic and transparent. Building trust within the community is essential. Be genuine, transparent, and honest in your interactions. Share your successes and failures, and be open to receiving feedback and constructive criticism.

5. Avoid self-promotion: While it's important to showcase your expertise, avoid excessive self-promotion within the community. Instead, focus on providing value and building relationships. Self-promotion should be done sparingly and in a way that adds value to the community.

7.2.5 Examples of Online Communities and Forums

HERE ARE SOME POPULAR online communities and forums that cater to home-based business owners:

1. Reddit: With numerous subreddits dedicated to entrepreneurship, small business, and specific industries, Reddit offers a wealth of knowledge and networking opportunities.
2. LinkedIn Groups: LinkedIn groups provide a platform for professionals to connect, share insights, and discuss industry-specific topics. Joining relevant groups can help you expand your network and stay updated on industry trends.
3. Facebook Groups: Facebook groups cover a wide range of topics and industries. Look for groups that align with your business niche and join those that have an active and engaged community.
4. Quora: Quora is a question-and-answer platform where entrepreneurs can ask questions, share their expertise, and connect with others in their industry.

Remember, the key to benefiting from online communities and forums is active participation and genuine engagement. By joining these communities, you can find support, gain knowledge, and build meaningful relationships that will contribute to the success of your home-based business.

7.3 Attending Networking Events

NETWORKING EVENTS ARE a valuable opportunity for home-based entrepreneurs to connect with like-minded individuals, expand their professional network, and gain valuable insights and knowledge. These events provide a platform for building relationships, exchanging ideas, and exploring potential collaborations. Attending networking events can be a powerful tool in your journey towards home-based success. In this section, we will explore the benefits of attending networking events and provide practical tips on how to make the most out of these opportunities.

7.3.1 The Benefits of Networking Events

NETWORKING EVENTS OFFER a range of benefits that can significantly impact your home-based business. Here are some key advantages to attending these events:

1. Building Relationships:

NETWORKING EVENTS PROVIDE a unique opportunity to meet and connect with other entrepreneurs, industry experts, and potential clients. Building strong relationships is essential for long-term success, and networking events offer a conducive environment for fostering these connections.

2. Knowledge Sharing:

ATTENDING NETWORKING events allows you to learn from experienced professionals and gain valuable insights into industry trends, best practices, and innovative strategies. These events often feature keynote speakers, panel discussions, and workshops that provide a wealth of knowledge and expertise.

3. Collaboration Opportunities:

NETWORKING EVENTS BRING together individuals from various industries and backgrounds, creating opportunities for collaboration and partnership. By connecting with complementary businesses or professionals, you can explore potential joint ventures, cross-promotions, or shared resources that can benefit your home-based business.

4. Increased visibility:

NETWORKING EVENTS PROVIDE a platform to showcase your expertise, products, or services to a targeted audience. By actively participating in conversations, sharing your knowledge, and engaging with others, you can raise awareness about your home-based business and attract potential clients or customers.

5. Support and encouragement:

BEING A HOME-BASED entrepreneur can sometimes feel isolating. Networking events offer a supportive community where you can connect with like-minded individuals who understand the challenges and triumphs of running a business from home. These events provide an opportunity to seek advice, share experiences, and find encouragement from others on a similar journey.

7.3.2 Tips for Maximizing Networking Events

ATTENDING NETWORKING events is not just about showing up; it's about making meaningful connections and leveraging the opportunities available. Here are some practical tips to help you make the most of networking events:

1. Set clear goals:

BEFORE ATTENDING A networking event, define your objectives. Are you looking to connect with potential clients, seek partnerships, or gain industry insights? Having clear goals will help you focus your efforts and make targeted connections.

2. Research the event:

TAKE THE TIME TO RESEARCH the networking event beforehand. Understand the event's theme, agenda, and the profiles of the speakers or attendees. This knowledge will enable you to identify individuals or sessions that align with your goals and make the most of your time at the event.

3. Prepare Your Elevator Pitch:

CRAFT A CONCISE AND compelling elevator pitch that effectively communicates who you are, what you do, and the value you offer. Practice delivering your pitch with confidence and clarity, ensuring that it resonates with your target audience.

4. Be approachable and engaging.

APPROACH NETWORKING events with a positive and open mindset. Smile, make eye contact, and be genuinely interested in others. Actively listen and ask thoughtful questions to show your engagement and build rapport with fellow attendees.

5. Bring ample business cards.

ENSURE YOU HAVE AN ample supply of business cards to exchange with other attendees. Your business card should include your name, contact information, and a brief description of your home-based business. This small but essential tool will help others remember you and follow up after the event.

6. Follow Up:

AFTER THE NETWORKING event, make it a priority to follow up with the individuals you connected with. Send personalized emails or LinkedIn messages to express your appreciation for the conversation and explore potential opportunities for collaboration or further discussion.

7. Be a resource:

NETWORKING IS NOT JUST about what you can gain; it's also about what you can offer. Be generous with your knowledge, insights, and connections. By being a resource to others, you build trust and establish yourself as a valuable member of the networking community.

8. Stay Active in Online Communities:

NETWORKING EVENTS DON'T end when the event is over. Stay active in online communities and forums related to your industry or niche. Engage in discussions, share valuable content, and continue building relationships beyond the physical event.

7.3.3 Types of Networking Events

NETWORKING EVENTS COME in various formats, catering to different preferences and objectives. Here are some common types of networking events you may consider attending:

1. Industry Conferences and Trade Shows:

THESE EVENTS BRING together professionals from a specific industry or niche. They often feature keynote speakers, panel discussions, and exhibition booths, providing ample opportunities for networking and learning.

2. Meetups and Workshops:

MEETUPS AND WORKSHOPS are informal gatherings where individuals with similar interests or goals come together to share knowledge and experiences. These events are usually smaller in scale, allowing for more intimate and focused networking.

3. Business Networking Groups:

BUSINESS NETWORKING groups are organized communities that meet regularly to exchange referrals, share business insights, and support one another. These groups often have a specific focus, such as women entrepreneurs, young professionals, or specific industries.

4. Social Events:

SOCIAL EVENTS, SUCH as cocktail parties or dinners, provide a more relaxed and informal setting for networking. These events allow for more casual conversations and relationship-building in a social atmosphere.

5. Online Networking Events:

WITH THE RISE OF VIRTUAL communication, online networking events have become increasingly popular. These events take place through webinars, virtual conferences, or online communities, allowing you to connect with professionals from around the world without leaving your home.

Conclusion

ATTENDING NETWORKING events is a powerful strategy for home-based entrepreneurs to expand their network, gain knowledge, and explore collaboration opportunities. By actively participating in these events and implementing the tips provided, you can maximize the benefits and accelerate your journey towards home-based success. Remember, networking is not just about what you can gain; it's about building meaningful relationships and being a resource to others in the digital jungle.

7.4 Finding Mentors and Coaches

IN THE FAST-PACED AND ever-changing world of home-based businesses, finding mentors and coaches can be a game-changer. These experienced individuals can provide guidance, support, and valuable insights that can help you navigate the challenges and achieve success in your entrepreneurial journey. Mentors and coaches can offer a fresh perspective, share their knowledge and expertise, and help you avoid common pitfalls. In this section, we will explore the importance of finding mentors and coaches and provide practical tips on how to connect with them.

7.4.1 The Value of Mentors and Coaches

MENTORS AND COACHES play a crucial role in the growth and development of home-based entrepreneurs. They have already walked the path you are embarking on and can provide valuable advice based on their own experiences. Here are some key benefits of having mentors and coaches:

Gaining knowledge and expertise

MENTORS AND COACHES have a wealth of knowledge and expertise in their respective fields. They can provide you with insights and strategies that can help you overcome challenges and make informed decisions. Their experience can save you time and effort by guiding you towards the most effective approaches.

Building confidence and motivation

STARTING A HOME-BASED business can be daunting, and self-doubt can creep in at times. Mentors and coaches can provide the encouragement and support you need to stay motivated and confident in your abilities. They can help you set realistic goals, celebrate your achievements, and keep you focused on your long-term vision.

Expanding Your Network

MENTORS AND COACHES often have extensive networks of professionals in various industries. By connecting with them, you gain access to their network, which can open doors to new opportunities, partnerships, and collaborations. They can introduce you to potential clients, suppliers, and other valuable contacts that can contribute to the growth of your business.

Accountability and feedback

MENTORS AND COACHES can hold you accountable for your goals and actions. They can provide constructive feedback and help you identify areas for improvement. Having someone to answer to can keep you on track and ensure that you are continuously growing and evolving as an entrepreneur.

7.4.2 Finding the Right Mentors and Coaches

FINDING THE RIGHT MENTORS and coaches is essential for maximizing the benefits they can provide. Here are some steps to help you find the right mentors and coaches for your home-based business:

Identify your needs and goals.

BEFORE SEEKING OUT mentors and coaches, take the time to identify your specific needs and goals. What areas of your business do you need guidance and support in? Are you looking for someone with expertise in marketing, finance, or operations? Clarifying your needs and goals will help you narrow down your search and find mentors and coaches who can provide the specific guidance you require.

Tap into your network.

START BY REACHING OUT to your existing network of contacts, friends, and colleagues. They may know someone who can be a potential mentor or coach for you. Attend industry events, conferences, and seminars to expand your network and meet professionals who can offer valuable insights. Online platforms and communities, such as LinkedIn and industry-specific forums, can also be great resources for finding mentors and coaches.

Research and evaluate potential mentors and coaches.

ONCE YOU HAVE IDENTIFIED potential mentors and coaches, conduct thorough research to learn more about their background, experience, and expertise. Look for individuals who have achieved success in their own businesses and have a track record of helping others succeed. Read their articles, books, or blog posts to get a sense of their approach and philosophy. It's also important to consider their availability and compatibility with your personality and working style.

Reach out and establish a connection.

WHEN REACHING OUT TO potential mentors and coaches, be respectful of their time and clearly articulate why you believe they would be a good fit for you. Explain your goals and how you believe their guidance can help you achieve them. Be genuine, and show your enthusiasm for learning from them. If possible, offer something of value in return, such as sharing your own expertise or assisting with a project they are working on.

Nurture the relationship.

ONCE YOU HAVE ESTABLISHED a connection with a mentor or coach, it's important to nurture the relationship. Be proactive in seeking their guidance and advice, but also be respectful of their time and boundaries. Show gratitude for their support and keep them updated on your progress. Remember that the relationship should be mutually beneficial, so look for ways to contribute to their success as well.

7.4.3 The Role of Mentors and Coaches in Different Stages of Business

MENTORS AND COACHES can be valuable at every stage of your home-based business journey. Here's how their role may evolve as your business grows:

Startup Stage

IN THE EARLY STAGES of your business, mentors and coaches can help you define your business model, set goals, and create a solid foundation. They can provide guidance on market research, product development, and establishing your brand identity. They can also help you navigate the challenges of starting a business and provide emotional support during this exciting but often overwhelming phase.

Growth Stage

AS YOUR BUSINESS STARTS to grow, mentors and coaches can assist you in scaling your operations, expanding your customer base, and optimizing your processes. They can help you identify new opportunities, develop marketing strategies, and manage your finances effectively. Their guidance can be instrumental in avoiding common pitfalls and ensuring sustainable growth.

Transition Stage

IF YOU ARE CONSIDERING expanding into new markets, launching new products, or making significant changes to your business, mentors and coaches can provide valuable insights and help you navigate the transition. They can offer guidance on strategic planning, risk management, and decision-making. Their experience can help you minimize risks and maximize the chances of success during periods of change.

Leadership Stage

AS YOUR BUSINESS MATURES and you take on a leadership role, mentors and coaches can help you develop your leadership skills, manage your team effectively, and maintain a healthy work-life balance. They can provide guidance on delegation, conflict resolution, and personal development. Their support can be invaluable as you navigate the challenges of leading a growing organization.

Conclusion

FINDING MENTORS AND coaches is a crucial step in achieving success in your home-based business. They can provide guidance, support, and valuable insights that can help you overcome challenges and reach your goals. By tapping into their knowledge and expertise, you can accelerate your growth, avoid common pitfalls, and build a thriving business. Take the time to identify your needs, tap into your network, and establish connections with mentors and coaches who align with your goals and values. Nurture these relationships and leverage their guidance at every stage of your entrepreneurial journey. Remember, success is not achieved in isolation, and having mentors and coaches by your side can make all the difference.

Overcoming Challenges and Achieving Success

8.1 Dealing with Isolation and Loneliness

Working from home can offer many benefits, such as flexibility, independence, and the ability to create your own schedule. However, one of the challenges that home-based entrepreneurs often face is the feeling of isolation and loneliness. Without the daily interactions and social connections that come with working in a traditional office setting, it's easy to feel disconnected from the outside world. In this section, we will explore strategies to help you deal with isolation and loneliness and create a harmonious work-life balance.

8.1.1 Understanding the Impact of Isolation and Loneliness

ISOLATION AND LONELINESS can have a significant impact on your mental and emotional well-being. It can lead to feelings of sadness, depression, and decreased motivation. When you work from home, you may miss out on the social interactions and support that come with working in a team or office environment. It's important to recognize the signs of isolation and loneliness and take proactive steps to address them.

8.1.2 Establishing a Routine

CREATING A DAILY ROUTINE can help combat feelings of isolation and loneliness. By establishing a structured schedule, you can create a sense of normalcy and purpose for your day. Start by setting regular working hours and sticking to them. This will not only help you stay focused and productive but also provide a sense of structure and routine. Additionally, make time for breaks and incorporate activities that promote social interaction, such as virtual coffee breaks with colleagues or networking events.

8.1.3 Engaging in Virtual Communities

ONE OF THE ADVANTAGES of the digital age is the ability to connect with others virtually. Take advantage of online communities and forums that cater to your industry or interests. Joining these communities can provide a sense of belonging and allow you to connect with like-minded individuals who understand the challenges and joys of working from home. Engage in discussions, ask questions, and offer support to others. By actively participating in virtual communities, you can combat feelings of isolation and build a supportive network.

8.1.4 Networking and Collaboration

WHILE WORKING FROM home may limit face-to-face interactions, it doesn't mean you can't network and collaborate with others. Attend virtual networking events, webinars, and conferences related to your industry. These events provide an opportunity to meet new people, exchange ideas, and potentially form partnerships or collaborations. Additionally, consider reaching out to other home-based entrepreneurs in your area and organizing meetups or co-working sessions. By connecting with others who are in a similar situation, you can share experiences, offer support, and combat feelings of isolation together.

8.1.5 Seeking Support from Family and Friends

YOUR FAMILY AND FRIENDS can be a valuable source of support when dealing with isolation and loneliness. Share your experiences and feelings with them, and let them know how they can support you. Schedule regular catch-ups or virtual hangouts with loved ones to maintain social connections. Additionally, consider involving your family and friends in your business by seeking their input or assistance. This not only strengthens your relationships but also provides a sense of collaboration and shared purpose.

8.1.6 Exploring Co-Working Spaces

IF YOU FIND THAT WORKING from home is becoming too isolating, consider exploring co-working spaces in your area. Co-working spaces provide a shared working environment where you can interact with other professionals.

They offer the benefits of a traditional office setting, such as networking opportunities, social interactions, and a sense of community. Co-working spaces can be a great option for those who crave the social aspect of working in an office but still want the flexibility of working from home.

8.1.7 Taking Breaks and Engaging in Self-Care

IT'S IMPORTANT TO PRIORITIZE self-care and take regular breaks throughout your workday. Use these breaks to engage in activities that promote relaxation and well-being. This could include going for a walk, practicing mindfulness or meditation, reading a book, or pursuing a hobby. Taking breaks not only helps to refresh your mind and increase productivity but also provides an opportunity to step away from work and combat feelings of isolation. Remember to prioritize your mental and emotional well-being as you navigate the challenges of working from home.

8.1.8 Seeking Professional Support

IF FEELINGS OF ISOLATION and loneliness persist and begin to impact your overall well-being, it may be beneficial to seek professional support. Consider reaching out to a therapist or counselor who can provide guidance and support. They can help you develop coping strategies, explore underlying issues, and provide a safe space to discuss your feelings. Remember, seeking professional help is a sign of strength, and it can greatly contribute to your overall well-being and success as a home-based entrepreneur.

In conclusion, dealing with isolation and loneliness is a common challenge for home-based entrepreneurs. By understanding the impact of isolation, establishing a routine, engaging in virtual communities, networking and collaborating, seeking support from family and friends, exploring co-working spaces, taking breaks, and seeking professional support when needed, you can overcome these challenges and create a harmonious work-life balance. Remember, you are not alone in this journey, and there are resources and strategies available to help you thrive in the digital jungle.

8.2 Managing Stress and Burnout

IN THE FAST-PACED AND demanding world of home-based businesses, stress and burnout can be common challenges that entrepreneurs face. The constant pressure to meet deadlines, juggle multiple tasks, and maintain a work-life balance can take a toll on one's mental and physical well-being. However, it is essential to recognize the signs of stress and burnout and implement effective strategies to manage and prevent them. In this section, we will explore various techniques and practices that can help you effectively manage stress and avoid burnout in your home-based business.

8.2.1 Recognizing the Signs of Stress and Burnout

STRESS AND BURNOUT can manifest in different ways, and it is crucial to be aware of the signs and symptoms. Some common indicators of stress and burnout include:

1. **Physical Symptoms**: Fatigue, headaches, muscle tension, sleep disturbances, and changes in appetite are some physical signs of stress and burnout. It is important to pay attention to these symptoms and address them promptly.

2. **Emotional Exhaustion**: Feeling overwhelmed, irritable, or experiencing mood swings can be signs of emotional exhaustion. It is essential to acknowledge and address these emotions to prevent them from escalating.

3. **Decreased Productivity**: When stress and burnout take hold, it can lead to a decline in productivity and motivation. If you find yourself struggling to focus or complete tasks efficiently, it may be a sign that you need to manage your stress levels.

4. **Isolation and Withdrawal**: Stress and burnout can also lead to social withdrawal and isolation. If you find yourself avoiding social interactions or feeling disconnected from others, it is important to address these feelings and seek support.

8.2.2 Implementing Stress Management Techniques

MANAGING STRESS IS crucial for maintaining a healthy and sustainable home-based business. Here are some effective techniques that can help you reduce stress and prevent burnout:

1. **Practice Self-Care**: Prioritize self-care activities such as exercise, meditation, and hobbies that bring you

joy and relaxation. Taking care of your physical and mental well-being is essential for managing stress.

2. **Set Realistic Expectations**: Avoid overcommitting and setting unrealistic expectations for yourself. Learn to delegate tasks, say no when necessary, and focus on what is most important to avoid feeling overwhelmed.

3. **Establish Boundaries**: Set clear boundaries between work and personal life. Create a designated workspace, establish specific working hours, and avoid checking work-related emails or messages outside of those hours. This will help you maintain a healthy work-life balance.

4. **Take Regular Breaks**: Incorporate regular breaks into your work schedule. Short breaks throughout the day can help refresh your mind and prevent burnout. Use this time to engage in activities that help you relax and recharge.

5. **Practice Stress-Relief Techniques**: Explore different stress-relief techniques such as deep breathing exercises, progressive muscle relaxation, or mindfulness meditation. These techniques can help you manage stress and promote a sense of calm.

6. **Seek Support**: Reach out to friends, family, or fellow entrepreneurs who can provide support and understanding. Joining online communities or networking groups can also provide a sense of camaraderie and help you connect with like-minded individuals facing similar challenges.

8.2.3 Preventing Burnout

PREVENTING BURNOUT is essential for long-term success in your home-based business. Here are some strategies to help you prevent burnout:

1. **Prioritize Self-Care**: Make self-care a non-negotiable part of your routine. Schedule regular exercise, healthy meals, and quality sleep to ensure you are taking care of your physical and mental well-being.
2. **Delegate and Outsource**: Identify tasks that can be delegated or outsourced to lighten your workload. Hiring freelancers or virtual assistants can help you focus on core business activities and reduce the risk of burnout.
3. **Practice Time Management**: Effective time management is crucial for preventing burnout. Prioritize tasks, set realistic deadlines, and avoid overloading your schedule. Remember to include breaks and downtime to recharge.
4. **Celebrate Achievements**: Take time to acknowledge and celebrate your accomplishments, no matter how small. Recognizing your achievements can boost motivation and prevent burnout by reminding you of the progress you have made.
5. **Continuous Learning and Growth**: Engage in continuous learning and personal development. Stay updated with industry trends, attend webinars or workshops, and seek opportunities to expand your knowledge and skills. This can help prevent

stagnation and keep you motivated.

6. **Regularly Assess and Adjust**: Regularly assess your workload, goals, and priorities. Be willing to make adjustments and adapt as needed. Flexibility and adaptability are key to preventing burnout and maintaining a healthy work-life balance.

Remember, managing stress and preventing burnout is an ongoing process. It requires self-awareness, self-care, and a commitment to maintaining a healthy work-life balance. By implementing these strategies and techniques, you can effectively manage stress, prevent burnout, and create a harmonious and successful home-based business.

8.3: Learning from Failure and Rejection

FAILURE AND REJECTION are inevitable parts of any journey towards success, and the world of home-based businesses is no exception. As an entrepreneur navigating the digital jungle, it is crucial to understand that setbacks and disappointments are not indicators of your worth or potential. Instead, they are opportunities for growth, learning, and resilience.

Embracing Failure as a Learning Experience

FAILURE IS OFTEN SEEN as a negative outcome, but it can be a powerful teacher if approached with the right mindset. Instead of dwelling on disappointment, successful home-based entrepreneurs view failure as a stepping stone towards improvement. They understand that each setback provides valuable lessons and insights that can be applied to future endeavors.

One of the first steps in learning from failure is to analyze what went wrong. Take the time to reflect on the situation and identify the factors that contributed to the outcome. Was it a lack of preparation, poor decision-making, or external circumstances beyond your control? By understanding the root causes, you can make adjustments and avoid repeating the same mistakes in the future.

It is also essential to embrace a growth mindset when faced with failure. Rather than viewing it as a personal flaw or a permanent setback, see it as an opportunity for growth and development. Embrace the idea that failure is not the end but a necessary part of the journey towards success. By reframing failure in this way, you can approach future challenges with resilience and determination.

Overcoming the Fear of Rejection

REJECTION IS ANOTHER common experience in the world of home-based businesses. Whether it's a potential client turning down your proposal or a publisher rejecting your book, it can be disheartening and demotivating. However, successful entrepreneurs understand that rejection is not a reflection of their worth or abilities. It is merely a part of the process.

To overcome the fear of rejection, it is crucial to separate your self-worth from the outcome. Remember that rejection is subjective and often based on factors beyond your control. Instead of internalizing the rejection as a personal failure, focus on the aspects that you can control and improve upon.

Developing resilience is key to bouncing back from rejection. Surround yourself with a supportive network of like-minded individuals who can provide encouragement and guidance during challenging times. Seek feedback from trusted mentors or peers to gain valuable insights into areas for improvement. Use rejection as an opportunity to refine your skills, enhance your offerings, and grow as an entrepreneur.

Learning and adapting

FAILURE AND REJECTION can be powerful catalysts for growth and innovation. They provide an opportunity to reassess your strategies, refine your approach, and adapt to the ever-changing digital landscape. Successful home-based entrepreneurs understand the importance of continuous learning and improvement.

One way to learn from failure and rejection is to conduct a thorough post-mortem analysis. Take the time to evaluate what worked and what didn't in your previous endeavors. Identify the patterns and trends that led to success or failure. Use this information to make informed decisions and adjustments in your future endeavors.

Additionally, staying updated with industry trends and best practices is crucial for adapting to the digital jungle. Attend conferences, webinars, and workshops to expand your knowledge and stay ahead of the curve. Engage in continuous learning through online courses, books, and podcasts to enhance your skills and expertise.

Cultivating resilience and perseverance

RESILIENCE AND PERSEVERANCE are essential qualities for navigating the challenges of the digital jungle. Building a successful home-based business requires determination, the ability to bounce back from setbacks, and the willingness to keep pushing forward.

To cultivate resilience, it is important to develop a strong support system. Surround yourself with individuals who believe in your vision and can provide emotional support during difficult times. Seek out mentors and coaches who can offer guidance and perspective. Engage with like-minded entrepreneurs who can share their experiences and insights.

In addition to a support system, self-care is crucial for maintaining resilience. Take time to recharge and rejuvenate, both physically and mentally. Prioritize activities that bring you joy and help you relax. Practice mindfulness and stress management techniques to stay centered and focused.

Remember, failure and rejection are not the end of your journey. They are stepping stones towards growth and success. Embrace them as opportunities to learn, adapt, and refine your strategies. Cultivate resilience, persevere through challenges, and celebrate the milestones and achievements along the way. In the digital jungle, harmony is found not by avoiding failure and rejection but by learning from them and using them as catalysts for growth.

8.4 Celebrating Milestones and Achievements

AS A HOME-BASED ENTREPRENEUR, it's important to take the time to celebrate your milestones and achievements along the way. Building a successful business from the comfort of your own home is no small feat, and recognizing your progress can help boost your motivation, morale, and overall satisfaction with your work. In this section, we will explore the importance of celebrating milestones and achievements, as well as provide some ideas on how to commemorate your successes.

8.4.1 The Importance of Celebrating

CELEBRATING MILESTONES and achievements is crucial for several reasons. First, it allows you to acknowledge the progress you have made in your home-based business. It's easy to get caught up in the day-to-day tasks and challenges, but taking a step back to reflect on how far you've come can provide a much-needed sense of accomplishment and fulfillment.

Secondly, celebrating milestones and achievements helps to maintain your motivation and drive. By recognizing your successes, you are reinforcing the belief that your hard work and efforts are paying off. This positive reinforcement can inspire you to continue pushing forward, even during challenging times.

Furthermore, celebrating milestones and achievements can also serve as a reminder of why you started your home-based business in the first place. It allows you to reconnect with your passion and purpose, reigniting your enthusiasm for your work.

8.4.2 Ways to Celebrate

THERE ARE NUMEROUS ways to celebrate your milestones and achievements as a home-based entrepreneur. The key is to find methods that resonate with you and align with your personal preferences. Here are some ideas to get you started:

8.4.2.1 Reflect and appreciate

TAKE SOME TIME TO REFLECT on your journey and appreciate the progress you have made. Write in a journal or create a gratitude list, noting down the milestones you have achieved and the lessons you have learned along the way. This exercise can help you gain perspective and cultivate a sense of gratitude for your accomplishments.

8.4.2.2 Treat Yourself

REWARD YOURSELF FOR reaching a milestone or achieving a significant goal. Treat yourself to something special, whether it's a small indulgence like a spa day or a weekend getaway. The reward should be meaningful to you and serve as a reminder that your hard work is paying off.

8.4.2.3 Share Your Success

SHARE YOUR ACHIEVEMENTS with your loved ones, friends, and fellow entrepreneurs. Celebrate with those who have supported you throughout your journey. This could be through a small gathering, a dinner party, or even a virtual celebration. Sharing your success not only allows you to bask in the joy of your achievements but also inspires and motivates others.

8.4.2.4 Create a vision board.

VISUALIZE YOUR FUTURE success by creating a vision board. Include images, quotes, and goals that represent your aspirations and dreams. Display it in your workspace as a constant reminder of what you have accomplished and what you are working towards.

8.4.2.5: Give Back

CONSIDER GIVING BACK to your community or a cause that is important to you. Celebrate your success by making a donation or volunteering your time and skills. Not only does this allow you to celebrate your achievements, but it also helps create a positive impact on others.

8.4.2.6 Document and Share

DOCUMENT YOUR MILESTONES and achievements through photos, videos, or blog posts. Share your journey with others, whether it's through social media, your website, or a newsletter. By documenting and sharing your successes, you not only celebrate your achievements but also inspire and motivate others who may be on a similar path.

8.4.3 The Power of Reflection

IN ADDITION TO CELEBRATING milestones and achievements, it's equally important to reflect on the lessons learned and the growth you have experienced. Reflection allows you to gain insights into your strengths and areas for improvement, enabling you to continue evolving and refining your home-based business.

Take the time to review your achievements and assess the strategies and actions that led to your success. Identify what worked well and what could be improved upon. This reflection process will not only help you celebrate your milestones but also provide valuable insights for future endeavors.

8.4.4 Setting New Goals

WHILE CELEBRATING MILESTONES and achievements is essential, it's also important to set new goals to keep your momentum going. Use your celebrations as a springboard for future success. Take the time to reassess your long-term vision and set new milestones and objectives that align with your evolving aspirations.

By continuously setting new goals, you ensure that you are always striving for growth and improvement. This ongoing process of setting and achieving goals will help you maintain your motivation and drive, propelling you towards even greater success in your home-based business.

8.4.5 Conclusion

CELEBRATING MILESTONES and achievements is a vital part of the home-based entrepreneurial journey. It allows you to acknowledge your progress, maintain motivation, and reconnect with your passion. By finding meaningful ways to celebrate, reflecting on your journey, and setting new goals, you can create a cycle of continuous growth and success. Embrace the opportunity to celebrate your milestones and achievements, and let them inspire you to reach even greater heights in your home-based business.

Also by imed el arbi

Metamorphosis Mindset: Transforming Your Life, One Thought at a Time
Life Mastery: a Toolkit for Success
Your Hidden Power of Mind: Unleashing Your Full Potential
Rise to Radiance
Realize Your Ultimate Potential
Revitalize Your Reality: The Art of Life Transformation
Transforming Within: A Path to Personal Evolution

YouTube Secrets
YouTube Secrets: Build a Successful Channel in 5 Days
YouTube Secrets: Build a Successful Channel with Artificial Intelligence
YouTube Secrets: the Ultimate Guide to Creating Popular and Successful Content

Standalone
The Magical Woodland Adventure

Shopify Mastery: The Ultimate Guide to E-commerce Success
Thriving Freelance: A Guide to Writing on Your Own Terms
Habit Mastery: A Simple Guide to Building Good Habits and Stopping Negative Ones
Reading Between the Gestures: A Brief Manual on Body Language
Bridges Across Cultures: Short story collection
Harmony in the Digital Jungle: Unveiling the Secrets of Home-Based Success
Cultivating Creativity: Fostering Innovation in Educational Settings
Gamification in Education: Leveling Up Learning Experiences
Mathematical Mastery: Unleashing the Power of Teaching
Smart Classrooms, Smarter Students: Navigating the AI Revolution in Education